Love on the LINE

Love on the LINE

How to Recover from Romance Scams Gracefully and Without Victimisation

Extended and Re-edited

ELINA JUUSOLA

Love on the Line

Copyright © 2019 by Elina Juusola. All rights reserved.

No part of this publication may be reproduced, stored in a retrieval system or transmitted in any way by any means, electronic, mechanical, photocopy, recording or otherwise without the prior permission of the author except as provided by USA copyright law.

The opinions expressed by the author are not necessarily those of URLink Print and Media.

1603 Capitol Ave., Suite 310 Cheyenne, Wyoming USA 82001
1-888-980-6523 | admin@urlinkpublishing.com

URLink Print and Media is committed to excellence in the publishing industry.

Book design copyright © 2019 by URLink Print and Media. All rights reserved.

Published in the United States of America
ISBN 978-1-64367-354-7 (Paperback)
ISBN 978-1-64367-353-0 (Digital)

1. Memoir
2. Self-Help
10.04.19

CONTENTS

INTRODUCTION..7
ACKNOWLEDGEMENTS 9

Chapter 1:   Introduction..11
Chapter 2:   My Story 18
Chapter 3:   The World through My Eyes 33
Chapter 4:   How are the Sex, Romance Book reading,
             and Pornography Industries Connected with
             the Romance Scams Industry? 40
Chapter 5:   How to Recognise Your Belief System 47
Chapter 6:   What to Know about the Chemistry of
             Love and Arousal 52
Chapter 7:   How to Use the Theory of Turning Emotion
             to Money and Develop a Perfect Pitch
             for Love for Scamming, Romance, and
             Pornography Industry Business.....................59
Chapter 8:   Why are Mature People More Vulnerable to
             Scamming?..65
Chapter 9:   Scammers 101: Unveiled 71
Chapter 10: Thinking about Recovery through
             Transformative Thinking...............................76
Chapter 11: Love Online: The Fairy Tale 87
Chapter 12: Discussion on the Possibility of Alternative
             Storylines through Social Change 92
Chapter 13: Love Online:
             The Alternative Short Story..........................99

Chapter 14: Concluding the Journey and
             Moving on with Life 107
Chapter 15: Tips for the Future Avoidance of Becoming
             a Victim of Fraud 110

APPENDIX: The Journey from Pioneer to Pathfinder 117
NOTES AND REFERENCES 131

INTRODUCTION

For the last 27 years we have observed the growth in cybercrimes from the days of CompuServe and America Online to today's trillion-dollar worldwide industry. Scams in all their forms have become a constant drain on society - a kind of Internet tax that siphons vast amounts of money from the global economy into a universe of criminal cartels not so different than that of drug trafficking. However, what is frequently overlooked is the cost in human lives—the victims of cybercrime.

Some cybercrimes have little impact on individual personal lives, a virus rarely affects someone personally other than a denial of access to their computers and technology, but some cybercrimes so profoundly impact their victims as to cause life-changing trauma that for many even leads to their death. This is the realm of online scams that do more than just collect vast amounts of money, they leave personal devastation in their wake.

As the Chairman of the major worldwide nonprofit nongovernmental organization that is focused on addressing both the criminality of online scams and the traumatized victims they leave behind, I am only too aware of the horrific effect on people's lives, families, and futures. Our organization hears every day in the voices of their victims how great the cost is of scams, such as romance scams, that pull their victims into a web of deep psychological manipulation and emotional destruction equal to that done to any battered spouse.

Our culture has barely begun to recognize the emotional cost and recovery challenges for these victims. Society's recognition of romance scam victims' trauma is at a stage similar to where awareness of sexual abuse trauma was 30 years ago. However, tremendous progress is being made by our organization, governments around the world, and recognized global scholars such as Elina Juusola.

We are immensely proud to count Elina Juusola as not only a founding-member of our organization, but also a member of our Board of Advisors for the work that she has done in both transforming her personal experience in these multi-national social engineering scams that profoundly affected her personally, but also for the ground breaking work she has done in helping develop models to directly help scam victims that we apply in our daily support of scam victims.

Juusola's work has benefitted countless romance scam victims around the world directly through her own face to face field work is supporting victims, but also in helping our organization to build better scam victims' assistance & support programs that have helped thousands of victims around the world. As a Senior Advisor to our organization [SCARS] she has been instrumental in helping us recognize the depth of the trauma victims experience and help us find ways to support victims that have yielded an over 30% success rate in recovery.

This book is not only Elina Juusola's astounding personal journey, but it is also a declaration of defiance to inspire all victims of romance scams and to show them a path into the light that for so many thought that there was no light left in their lives. This is a watershed work that will be recognized both for the moment in which it emerged but also for setting the tone for our own combined work to turn around the lives of so many tragically affected by these devastating psychologically manipulative crimes. We urge every scam victim to read this book and share it.

October 11, 2018

Tim McGuinness, Ph.D.
Founder & Chairman
Society of Citizens Against Romance Scams [SCARS]
Miami, Florida, U.S.A.
www.AgainstRomanceScams.org
contact@AgainstRomanceScams.org

ACKNOWLEDGEMENTS

Many people and circumstances have contributed to my writing of this book. First and foremost, this book would not have come about without the grass-roots women's movement I was part of during the last thirty plus years. The freedom of thinking and acting for women and for global peace has contributed to my convictions about the world. These ideas have been grounded in me through my mentors in the women's movement including, among others, Ingegerd Lundström, Dale Spender, Amy Kaminsky, Berit Ås, Hilkka Pietilä, the late Kari Mattila, Wilma Scott-Heide, Else Barth, and Joan Rothchild.

My heartfelt thanks to wonderful Gloria Orenstein for seeing in my manuscript much more than I did at first and writing the appendix to this book.

I can also thank those who contributed to my theosophical upbringing, especially my late grandfather, Olavi Palo, and my early mentor Joy Mills.

There is a dear friend who has played the crucial part in writing this book. I want to thank Chris Henderson, her Unstoppable Women coaching group, and her Women Howling at the Moon community in Brisbane. Her commitment has restored in me the belief that I am not alone and that there are plenty of women out there taking action in changing the world. Her connections have also contributed to me having a wonderful group of women to rely on for comments. These include Maria Roeckmann and Lani Morris. I want to thank my very good friends Denise Arbabzadah, Salme Durbin, Eeva Gopaul, Glenda Heig, and Sandra Vincent-Gay, who have supported me through the writing process.

I thank the Queensland Police Fraud Prevention and Support Group or their encouragements, especially Angela Tilbrook who, in addition to becoming a friend, kept sending me the most encouraging emails while she read the manuscript.

I want to thank my sons, Hanno and Nillo they live on the other side of the world from me, but our fun conversations and imagined movie scripts about romance scams prompted the whole idea of the book in my head.

Last but not least, I want to thank my daughters, Henna and Nelli for being there for me through the writing process and my wonderful grandchildren, Iida, Hera, Henry, Tessa, Hilla and Olli for restoring in me the spirit of generational exchange and the courage to think that there is a great future in store for humanity despite all the odds.

CHAPTER 1

Introduction

"I could never find anyone as special as you are, Elina. I love you so much."

If you received a text like the above sentence, would you not feel good? Would it not make you smile, just a little, inside your heart? Well, I received one, and it made me smile. It was the parting text from my online love interest—just before I blocked him from all my contacts.

The idea of writing this book came to me because I was scammed by a very professional and seasoned man on the Internet. After innocently filling in a form offered on Facebook for an Internet dating site called Be2, I was contacted by not one but two people, both of whom turned out to be scammers.

The first one fell into the category I was familiar with and had been previously warned about—the person who is pretending to be something they obviously aren't. In this case, my would-be date was supposedly an Irish-born engineer with a small child, who lived and worked in Texas but who had no English-language skills. The second one wrote in regular English; he even responded to jokes as naturally as he responded to anything else I wrote about. I really thought he was a winner.

In fact, I thought that he was absolutely fantastic—until I started suspecting him to be a scammer. About a month into the affair, he started asking for money. However, by then I had deemed him a genuine and an intelligent guy, so I went along with the first request. When he then supposedly got into more and more trouble, I started doing my research. At the same time, I absolutely loved the attention and was quite reluctant to let the relationship go.

Even though I consider myself to be a fairly smart person, I still fell for it. As I was beginning to wonder if something was amiss, I had several conversations with my friends about Internet dating. I was surprised to learn that most of them had experienced online dating themselves.

These coffee-club talks with friends and acquaintances revealed that many of them had, in fact, been in the same situation as I was. While some had met their partner or lover online, others had also been scammed. Some of them had experienced this many times. What was most astonishing was that they had never really talked about their experiences before. Our conversations revealed that many were still traumatised by the events they described. Most revealed that they were still clearly angry when remembering the incidents. I immediately undertook further study to find ways to help the victims of scams— including myself. The data I was able to collect revealed to me that Internet romance scams are on the rise worldwide.

In 2013, dating and romance scams topped the list of financial scams in Australia. The Australian Competition and Consumer Commission (ACCC) figures show that in that year, 2,777 reports for romance fraud were submitted; out of those, 1,189 people lost money—altogether as much as $23 million.[1]

The figures for losses in the United States and the United Kingdom are even more outrageous. In 2012 in the United States, people reportedly lost nearly $56 million to scammers through romance scams, and in the United Kingdom, the total was £24 million.[2] I was fascinated by the research that was undertaken at the University of Leicester in the United Kingdom about the psychology of online dating. It struck me quite hard.

It stated that in 2012, about 230,000 people in the United Kingdom "may have fallen" for romance scams. What really affected me was that out of all the participants in this study, none had actually recovered from the effects the scam had on them.[3] That finding immediately gave me a reason to start looking for a possible solution. I also searched different media outlets for relevant clues. In particular, Australian ABC and SBS channel documentaries offered the best source for information.

In August 2014 there was a documentary series called *Head First* introduced by Sabour Bradley on the Australian ABC TV network.[4] Part one of the first series, about online scammers from Ghana, was called "The Social Monster." The episode had an interesting storyline that highlighted the different ways in which scammers manipulate their victims into sending them money despite great difficulties in the victims' own lives. That particular story had a positive resolution; some of the scammers were caught, thanks to the efforts of the Queensland Police, Sabour Bradley, and the Ghana Police Service working together.

Ghana seems to have a high population of scammers, and while scamming is officially condemned, it is pretty much considered part of the everyday culture of their society. This also applies to other African countries, such as Nigeria. You only need to Google "Ghana scam" or "Nigerian scam," and the descriptions are there for you to read. By the time I had discovered this, I was already making connections in my mind between scamming and pornography and romance books. It finally hit me while I was watching the last program in the second series of *Heads First*. This episode, "The Porn Ultimatum," explored the porn culture online and in the open market. I realised that the phenomenon of scamming falls within the same patterns I was familiar with from researching pornography and violence against women. With that revelation, the world made sense to me once again. By taking my clues from the same research I had left behind so long ago, I was now able to explain and interpret these unexpected commonalities.

Sabour's closing comment struck me the most:

> We are all in a relationship with porn—and there *is* a price to pay. It can be destructive, it's gonna get more extreme and access is way too easy. But those

are separate issues to the effect it is having on our relationships. Blaming [something else] on those breakdowns seems far easier than standing up, like Ken and most of the addicts I met and admitting it is masking a void in us or our relationships and we are using it to fill that void. So, instead of blaming the porn, shouldn't we be looking into the void? Problem is, we all know what happens when we do that.[5]

This started me thinking about my own life experiences. I have gained a great deal of knowledge from fifteen years of researching and speaking about sex, pornography, prostitution, and violence against women during the 1980s and 1990s. My findings fit with this new development and the opportunities the Internet has brought for entrepreneurial criminals. I decided that it was time to share my experience.

As a historian of ideas, my main research in pornography was always focused on the messages it delivers and the underlying theory behind those messages. I used to have ongoing arguments with many audiences about the relativity of the following belief: We are all in a relationship with pornography, and the masculine culture we live in mirrors that theory in ways that make uncovering the deception behind the ideas basically impossible if we do not get rid of the whole idea of "porne."[6]

After those fifteen years of research and touring the world during the eighties and nineties, I became disillusioned with the world we live in. I made a conscious effort—with varying levels of success—*not* to follow the debate on the subject; however, after my own experience with online dating and scams, I felt that I should rethink my position. I knew that the message I could deliver would be important enough that I should share my experience with an Internet scam. I felt it would be important enough to be helpful to humanity. In addition, I was quite confident that I had found a way to help myself recover from the trauma all on my own. I felt it important to share my positive and empowering approach into the retrieval from the ordeal.

I want to share my experience as encouragement to others that recovery is possible. I have two distinctive aims with this book.

If we look at romance scams in the larger context of sex, pornography, and the development of the romance-book industry over the last thirty years, we can see the link to the seeming inequality in the world. If we see romance scams as mirroring the history of violence—period—that makes it possible and so easy to set stereotypes and opposing warlike frameworks that justify the gaining of money and power for some over others. Any way we look at it, these kinds of contradictions enable an open field of possibilities for the exploitation of some human beings. I have been captivated by the idea of finding these connections for the last thirty years. The romance scam experience adds another dimension to what I had already suspected.

However, this presentation is not an academic or a scientific discourse. Rather, it is a story of my personal experience in linking together the patterns of my previous research. Thus my second aim is to provide a popularised reflection of the issue at hand, explained with the help of my past experiences as a researcher in the field of sex, pornography, and violence against women. Nonetheless, I have undertaken some further research in support of the convictions that are brought forward in this book.

In the coming chapters, I will compare what the satisfaction of reading romance books, watching porn, or looking at graphic novels (comics) have in common with falling for that unknown person at the end of the line. I will reflect on how the scammers have learned from other industries and combined that knowledge in their business structure. Further on, I will consider the world at large around us and the fact that there still is such lingering inequality of wealth and power between the different parts of that world that it divides us into poor and rich as basis for stereotyping. I will also look deeper into the realm of persuasion as a technique for online scam that enables the scammers to be so effective in their goal of parting targets from their money.

In the context of the big themes, my first aim is to answer the question of why, in this world with its aging population, mature people are particularly targeted and vulnerable to exploitation and scams. In relation to this, I also want to explore some interesting theories about how the chemistry of love and arousal works in relation to a professional approach that induces people to give and send money to those strangers who we have not met in real life—just on the basis of raised emotion. I want to see whether this is more applicable to mature people than to other groups. The latter part of the book introduces a positive and creative method

I have developed to be used for recovery from the trauma caused by a romance scam. In the course of writing this book, I have found many theories that propound the idea that writing or artistic pursuits can be a great way to recover from post-traumatic stress. In the case of romance scams, I have found that this can be done by embracing the positive emotions that were caused by the romantic side of the online affair and by writing out the best romance according to the victim's imagination— thus separating the criminal from the fantasy, just as in the world of romance fiction. In conclusion, I have also included my own experiences of the process of writing the best possible romance story I could.

How to Use this Book

This book provides a way to make sense of why anyone, intelligent and educated or not, can fall for a romance scam online.

I find it a real shame that scammers get away with the crime, and victims suffer and keep suffering as the incident (which typically lasts only a couple of months) carries on in their minds and affects their lives—maybe even until they die. It is a waste of time to let the scammers get the best of us and win. Let's turn that around.

The positive and empowering method I came to use for my own recovery is introduced in this book. It aims to assist in quick recovery from the trauma and is based on embracing the situation and directing the raised emotions to creative process for self-empowerment.

Use this Book to

- understand the larger context of violence in which the romance scams belong
- understand how the scammers, even the ones who work alone, are part of the human trafficking industry that collects the largest amount of money in the world apart from the drug industry;
- separate the criminal and the romance from each other to avoid being sucked right back in the second time around;
- add value to the experience by keeping the positive emotional experience andredirecting it into creativity for self-empowerment;
- share by publishing your stories for others to read and be warned what kind of scams are being presented;
- help you gain closure for yourself;
- get on with your life.

CHAPTER 2

My Story

> Long life for, long life for erotism,
> Long life for, long life for erotism,
> It's time, it's time. It's time for erotism.
> You couldn't turn me on, the night you wanted to take me;
> You couldn't turn me on, for paper girls fake me,
> For illusion, illusion, illusion in my sexuality.

There is no real profile for a person who would fall under the spell of an Internet romance scammer. The UK research has shown that there really are not any particular types of people who are more vulnerable than others. The research into people who fall for scammers' tricks did not support the predetermined assumptions.[1]

Reading books and articles, or even updating my research on pornography and the sex industry, did not satisfactorily explain to me why I fell under the spell of a professional scammer—yet I did. I could, however, see that at the time I might have been more susceptible due to depression following my mother's death and my attempts to manage the pain of fibromyalgia.

In hindsight, I can see that I needed something to distract me from my suffering, and that led me to sensation-seeking. I tried travel, but it did not help me to bounce back. Consequently, the online dating scam was perhaps just as suitable a way to wake me back up to the world; however, I did not ask for it or expect it at all.

Answering a message sent by a person who claimed to be from Alice Springs, in the Northern Territory in Australia, did not seem such a big thing, but what followed was.

1.

Hello Elina, Thanks for sending me your email address on Be2, how is the weather like in Brisbane today? Please let me know if you get this email and I will write you more about myself and also email you some more pictures of me. I will be waiting to hear from you soon.

Stephen.[2]

Hi Stephen,
   It is an absolutely sunny morning here in Brisbane. A bit cold though, so tough job to rise from the bed as it is the warmest place.
   I did get your email, thank you! Looking forward to conversing with you.

A very normal start to the conversation with anyone, I would say. I asked him why he had not uploaded his picture online. I reasoned that he was a lawyer or someone important in Alice Springs and did not want people to recognise him from an online dating site. Turns out he had another story altogether.

2.

Hello Elina,
   I am very happy you got my email; l will like to tell you some more about myself. Well, with a dual citzenship (British-Australian) I am Stephen. I was born and bred in Alice Springs many years ago by an Australian mother nurse called Helen and a British father called Phil. My parents met at the university …

He told me how his parents had died and how he had had to move to the United Kingdom to live with his uncle and had joined the army there, following his uncle's example. He described how he had had a hard time understanding the strict discipline his uncle had forced on him as a teenager but how he had coped with it. He told me that he was currently serving in the peacekeeping force stationed in Afghanistan but would soon return home to the UK with the British troops. He said he was a major general looking for someone with whom to share his life after retirement.

I felt really empathetic towards him. It was a very nice email, and he said things about friendship that really affected me. It was not into analysing the form of the language, just conversing with another human being. I am from a non-English background myself, so judging the English grammar would not even have been possible for me. I felt he was sincere. In fact, I commended him on it afterwards. Most importantly, I wanted to get to know this person better.

He said that he had not uploaded his picture because it was not good practice for the military to be on dating sites and he did not want people to know about it. He sounded lonely. He concluded with this:

I don't request for anything than loving and happy committed relationship with someone special. I'm not a fighter and I don't argue, life is too short but I do value friendship and intimacy. Respect is one of the most important requisites in a relationship, as are honesty and commitment.

I believe neither of us really thought that we would meet someone special online but it just come to pass, partly thanks to our personality description through which we learned a few things about each other. I was ready to fall in love with someone special whoever that happens to be. There are few qualities which talks about genuine woman in relationship, such as faithfulness, loyalty, trustworthy, honesty, respectful etc.

I guess having those qualities in relationship can really help a lot. I am not looking to fill a void in my life; I am looking for my soulmate. I consider myself a very easygoing person, an even-tempered one. Do you have Skype messenger so we could chat on there sometimes and get to know each other better. I hope you like my pictures? I will be waiting to hear from you soon.

Stephen.

It takes a really suspicious person to always try to find fault with what anyone writes or says. I am not like that at all. In fact, I had decided long ago, after researching pornography and human trafficking, that trying to keep a façade of oneself, building an image that would appeal to others, was a severe waste of energy and that I would generally take people at face value. This might not be the best advice for people meeting online, but it has worked for me until the Internet age changed how people met.

"Stephen" sent me pictures of himself, both military and civil pictures. One was of "him" sitting at the famous site The Rocks in Afghanistan. At that time I did not know that the pictures had been stolen from a well-known source. Only after finding them on a Facebook site[3] did I realise that some poor person's identity had been used to scam me. But I had decided to go out of my comfort zone from the beginning, and I had two lovely girls at home encouraging me to answer his mail. So I did:

Hi Stephen,

> Thanks for your message.
> Wow! It was a bit of a shock to get to know that you are in Afghanistan and actually live in UK. I do like your earnestness about your life though.
> I do come to London sometimes …

I told him about my family in Finland, in the United Kingdom, and all over the world. I described how I was used to travelling and having long-distance relationships. I felt that there was a real connection there, but of course that was the whole point of his agenda. How could I have predicted that? I was just excited that I had met someone who would be OK to converse with and share some experiences with. And his answer came post-haste.

3.

Hello Elina,
> Thanks for the reply. I hope you had a wonderful weekend? I am happy you don`t have any problem with the distance between us at the moment. This means meeting each other after I am out of here wouldn't be a problem at all. Let me tell you some more about myself …

He told me about how he had lost his parents and about his marriage that had ended ten years earlier when his wife and daughter were lost in a car crash. Afterwards his work had gotten him through the sorrow. He also told me that he would like an animal to care for after retirement. He finished with this:

> I am a person who is very real when it comes to life and its issues. I am honest, kind, caring, and affectionate, have a good sense of humour. I am easygoing, a free thinker, trustworthy and respect the lives of other people.
>
> I'm excited to see new places, meet new people and do new things … I'm fascinated with the world and different cultures and would enjoy learning more about them … I love to laugh and like being around people with a good sense of humour.

He sounded like fun. I was immediately charmed by his words. Of course, I now know that they were a combination of various emails that many people get on online dating sites. Words have a huge effect on the reading audience. In fact, reading romance novels is a huge turn-on for millions of women and men. If you look into the romance book industry, you see a great change towards a more and more professional way of writing. There are trends to follow and styles to consider. The continuous-improvement plan lies in the modern approach to training that concentrates on coaxing larger audiences to follow an author by persuading them that the next book is even better that the last. The competition for the buying audience is fierce; the digital world has made it so easy for everyone to consume. But did I think of that when I read Stephen's words? No, I was affected by the image. And when I did not answer quickly enough, he prompted me, and I answered.

Hi Stephen,

Yes, I did get your email. I have had quite a busy day today and haven't had time yet to respond.

I checked that there is five and a half hours' difference in time between Kabul and Brisbane.

Did you take yourself off the be2 site as I did not find your message there any more? I was going to check on your Skype address …

I asked him if he had met some other nice women through the dating site, as I knew that often a man his age wanted to marry a younger woman and start a family in retirement. I would not mind, I said.

I am asking you these questions so that you do not feel that you have to be obligated to me even though you are writing to me. You don't have to be exclusive here because it might be that you found some another women to converse with as well who might be more suitable partners to you in the future. I am very happy to converse with you and see how we are getting along and if we really have the chemistry you talked about before though. Anyway, you get points from me right away in that you are interested in mature women ...

And I did send him a picture of me with my granddaughter, playing a song together.

4.

Hello Elina

Thanks for the email. I really enjoyed reading it and seeing the picture, very lovely. You are right about the time difference between us Elina. It is almost midnight here and I won`t be having any sleep tonight because I am in the monitoring room here on camp helping my men on patrol track down some Taliban hideout and also to alert them if there is any danger. I had to take off my profile from the Internet because I didn`t want to get into trouble with my superiors. I am not allowed to be on a dating site while on duty. I wasn`t having any luck on there either. Now that I have met you I hope we stay in touch and see how things go between us. Do not worry about the age gap, it doesn`t bother me at all ...

He told me that he did not want any more kids, just someone to share his life after retirement. I felt reassured and thought the email was very sweet. In fact, it was turning out that I felt the same way I felt after reading my favourite romance books. I felt high as the endorphins produced by my brain started affecting me. It is much better on paper than face to face, as the words are there to be read again and again, and the effect is the same, every time. He finished with this:

I am happy your daughter encouraged you to keep in touch with me, I can`t wait to find out how things go between you and I soon. I am taking care of myself here and

God is always in control of our lives here meaning me and other troops under my control. He is going to make everything up to us in the best ways so we would be forever happy. Amen! Never stop praying for every other troop here as I very much believe in prayers. I will be thinking about you. Hugs and kisses.

And so the story goes. We established a relationship in fifteen days, after which he completely changed over to Skype, phone conversations, and texting, while I kept sending him emails. The following is his last email:

I want to say thank you so much for the lovely mails and pictures you keep sending me. I really appreciate them as they make my day brighter. It was great talking to you on the phone, you take my breath away Elina. I really enjoyed hearing your voice so loud and clear and can't wait to hear it again soon. I am glad that you also have such strong feelings for me Elina because I wouldn`t know what I would have done if I was the only one feeling this way. I give you my word I am going to always love and care for you, treat you with respect and make you happy always because you mean the world to me now ...

By that time I was sold, of course. Who would not be, after such intensive emailing back and forth? As well, I recalled that my grandmother had also had a long-distance relationship, from Finland to Australia, which had lasted for three years and which resulted in her travelling around the world and finally marrying her pen friend in 1967. In the digital age we had completed the equivalent of perhaps months or years of such international letter-writing in just fifteen days. This was greatly amusing, I thought, and so did my online friend.

I set the terms for our texting. I told him that I had never in my life texted amorously with anyone. I expressed that I would absolutely love the experience, and he delivered, every time. You could see that our texting was done on two levels, which assured me that this man was really intelligent, as he could understand allegory and spoke either poetically and passionately or normally, as required, and we both knew the difference. He even understood my dad's best dirty joke from Lapland and reacted spontaneously and rapturously to it in his text. This further assured me that he was who he said he was. Here are some examples:

Stephen: "My love can you please come on Skype now. I've missed you so much Elina."

Stephen: I hope you get this text Elina. I am facing a serious situation here and going through a hard time here babe. I am missing you here so much and can't wait.
Me: Kisses and hugs to you, my love. I am really sorry to hear that. I feel for you, so much. I believe in you, Stephen. Love from Elina.
Stephen: I am going to do everything in my power to make sure this problem is sorted and we are finally together soon. I love you so much and missing you here badly.
Me: You have a cool head, Stephen. I know that you will find a solution. You simply must. For us. I love you. I will be back tomorrow night. And will write to you, then.
Me: Honestly, Stephen. I cannot wait for you to walk through my door. We will have so much fun. And so much love.
Stephen: I can't wait to be with you Elina so am doing everything in my power to sort this once and for all so we can start our new life together.
Me: I just know that you will be successful, Stephen. You are a marvel and a blessing to me.

Stephen: Elina, I love you because you bring the best out of me.

Me: Hello Stephen, my love. Just sending you hugs and kisses before I sleep. Elina.

Stephen: Thanks so much for the text my love. I hope you dream about me Elina.

Many kisses and hugs to you. Goodnight.

Me: So, did your Internet go down Stephen? Lots of hugs and kisses to you.
Stephen: Yes my love. They are trying to fix it now, would let you know when it's working.

Stephen: "It seems the Internet is not going to start working anytime soon so I have to return to the house now. I want you to know that I love you so much Elina. Kisses and hugs.
Me: Lots of love to you. I will do the affirmation again. You are so good at heightening my vibrational levels. We are so lucky!
Stephen: "Yes we are and would surely be happily together soon. I love you with all my heart, body and soul. Many kisses and hugs to you my sweetheart.

We also had many conversations on Skype, and they would vary from just saying hello to being somewhat sexy. Nothing major in terms of what many romance and other books would have, but taken in the context at that particular moment, it was arousing and further assurance that he could get the job done in real life in a mature manner. And my proof of this affair being just like a romance book was that I had not read any romance books during it. The connection provided me with enough highs to be distracted from both pain and boredom.

I talked about him all the time to my family. They were happy for me, as they could see that I was happy. My elder daughter was a little bit sceptical, but my younger came to my defence and told my elder daughter that he was calling me on the phone, so he was clearly a real person.

I tested my limits as to how much he would take in terms of what I would write to him, and he accepted everything, without question, unconditionally. How fantastic! Once I wrote to him about *tantra* and then got anxious. He called me and laughed. That was a turning point, as I felt that I truly could tell him everything.

His raspy and very low-toned voice was fantastic. It sounded like he had broken his voice somehow, but the effect on me was huge. Having previously been diagnosed with fibromyalgia, a nervous-system disorder, and soft-muscle arthritis, I had suffered from pain every day for a long time. His voice did a sort of miracle; hearing him speak on the phone directly affected my nervous system, and the burning eased. "It is psychological," commented my eldest daughter, but to me it happened for real. I told him so, and he called even more.

Then my Stephen went on the promised last mission to Afghanistan, and the storyline began to deteriorate.

The story he gave was that he had sent his belongings through Dubai to the United Kingdom, with a UN agent. The package was being held at Dubai customs. Would I help with the money to pay for the customs papers? He couldn't do it himself, as the package contained his illegally acquired "reward" from the Afghan government, and he did not want the MoD (British Ministry of Defence) to know about it. I did help him there. I figured that anybody could do things like that without thinking of the consequences. People in higher positions had more opportunities for temptation than others in lower ranks. I did it, but this was not enough.

Customs wanted the High Court to clear the forms, but I could not help with that. His character got into more trouble. He was anxious about them scanning the package and wanted to leave Afghanistan, which he did. Suddenly I got a call from Ghana.

By that time I had become suspicious, despite him having provided me with several different forms of identification. What actually made me send his details to my son to look into was the fact that I had asked him to send me his credentials, which were supposedly provided by the British Army, and somehow they did not convince me.

Actually, prior to that he had warned me himself not to research him online, as I "might find people telling bad things" about him. He kept telling me how he did not want to lose me over it. Only in hindsight did this seem "off" to me. At the time I accepted his warning at face value.

Then my son uploaded his information online; in a couple of minutes he found "Stephen" and sent me a link. His comment was, "Mom, here are the links, but you don't need to read them. That way you can remember only how he has romanced you. It is not necessary to read all the dirt people are writing about him."

I followed my son's advice, but I did not block "Stephen." I thought that by keeping the conversation going, I might be able to help the police arrest him in the end. However, that did not happen. Instead, I wanted to find out how he had tricked me. Our conversation continued and became more intellectual as we went on to discuss and experiment with various visualisation techniques and other theories about how to transmute the emotion of romance into creativity as per my suggestion to do so. This continued until I had researched enough about Internet scams to get really worried for my family. In a couple of weeks I was ready to report him to ACCC and the police as his character's situation was threatening to worsen in Accra.

Afterwards, when I checked the reports on him, I found that many of the reports, despite the loss of money, were actually favourable when it came to his ability to romance women. Here are two examples from the site:

Kenneth (or whatever his name is) made contact with me and asked to contact directly via email and soon progressed to Skype. Although we tried to video link up, we could only view and not speak. Within the first few emails he was writing love letters—very romantic and what every lady likes to hear[4]

I met him on Chemistry, he says he is in the British services stationed there, he seems very romantic says all the things you want to hear, but when something is too good to be true time to check it out[5]

My experience in reporting this crime to ACCC and police should also be told here, as it was possibly more upsetting to me than the whole scam. After all, the scammer possibly saved my life by waking me up to my own emotions, and I felt that I had participated quite sufficiently in my own fall to deserve losing the money. However, reporting the incident got me really angry.

I spent a whole morning on the phone to different government institutions, including the Queensland Police, and got absolutely nowhere with it. I felt that if I had not been so insistent, I would have been thoroughly traumatised, for sure.

At first I called the ACCC's www.scamwatch.gov.au, as instructed. A nice call-centre representative first told me to report it online but then took my report herself anyway. Then she connected me to a helpline, as I wanted to know whether I could help with police.

The helpline representative clearly did not understand either my accent or my intention, as she kept insisting that I would not be able to recover my money. Usually it was impossible, she insisted, no matter how much I had lost, but since I *had* lost money, I should report the crime to Queensland Police. So I visited to my local police station, as instructed.

The Queensland Police receptionist at my local station said that it was not their issue, as the crime was international, and she went to the back office to find out what else I could do. After I had waited a long time, a nice young man came out and handed me a piece of paper that listed contact numbers to the Federal Police. I called one. That got me a recorded message that went from one number to the next until the call was cut off. I called the other number provided, and the person answering that advised me that I should call the Queensland Police main number. I did so.

There the representative instructed me to go to my local police. After I explained that I had already done so, he advised me that they should have the process in their Operational Standard File and that the person in charge should know about it. Then he proceeded to read me all the information in their book, which was brilliant, as I ended up back at the same website[6] as before, to where I then reported the whole scam, to the international police, I presume.

No one ever phoned me or indicated that they were interested, and everywhere it was lamented that I would not be able to recover my money. Nor, it seemed, was anyone really interested in the fact that it was a crime, that the scammer should be arrested, and that I might be able to help.

From my perspective, I could not be bothered to do more than I did there. I was pretty much done with the system. As I see it, the bigger picture is the one I am interested in. I was never really into finding out who my scammer was or where he came from, as in my world view I have always concentrated on long-term results. To me it is not necessary to victimise the individual scammers of the world or even punish them. What I see as important is to understand the patterns built into our behaviour that contribute to how susceptible people are and how easy it is to manipulate them. I would like to add to the knowledge and understanding of why it is so and help to make the world a bit more honest place for the humanity in the long run. It does not have to be in my lifetime.

Then, seeing the *Heads First* program on ABC TV prompted me to call the Queensland Police number and enquire whether the support group that was said to be there was actually still active. It took around two weeks, and then I received a call from the detective senior constable, inviting me to a support group the next day.

Of course I went there and have continued to go along, despite the fact that my first experience at the group aroused really confusing thoughts in my mind. That could be because the group was still so much of an experiment that a newcomer might feel real abandonment and confusion. Nevertheless, to participate within the goodwill of a group helps to understand the processes and to become more self-confident. The atmosphere of the group is truly supportive for those who need it after such a harrowing experience as a romance scam can be. The group has "grown on me," as they say, and I now understand better why people go to a group at all. I would like to see more people there though. Afterwards I kept asking myself what I had learned from my experience. Honesty with myself brought me to the conclusion that my thought patterns had been falling into a downward spiral for a while. I would say that this had been my situation for the previous three or four years and that it probably contributed to my being so unprepared to investigate further the identity of my online "friend." This was the result of a few factors coming together.

First of all, for a long time I had felt stressed and unsupported in my work as a director for a community organisation. I had felt not well appreciated and had run out of solutions for myself. So I had gone with the least terrible option and quit.

My company felt that they owed me something and paid me some money for my trouble. That enabled me to go travelling around the world and to have some lovely experiences. However, just as I was ready to start back on my regular life, my mother had died suddenly. The day before she passed away, something went wrong with my nervous system, and from then on my life kept deteriorating so that in the end I was in continuous pain. My thoughts deteriorated until I believed that there was nothing there to live for; instead of my 110-year plan, my life would be over at 60.

Nothing helped. Bad news kept coming my way. I did start therapy, and I found line dancing. But even travelling didn't help any more. I actually kept myself going by constantly reading romance books—the more hard-core the better. The positivity of my friends did not help; my business success did not help. Everything felt dead in me.

Then, out of the blue, the Be2 ad caught my eye on Facebook, where they said that people over forty-five could join free. I filled in the form. And just like that, I was in a full online affair, so quickly that it took me by surprise. But I felt happy with it, and basically, my family was supporting me because it made me so happy.

Then it was over. I realised that it was a scam and had to end it, because it was supporting criminals. But I learned something vital in the process—something that I had not learned over my thirty-five years of researching pornography, violence against women, and the sex industry and its connections to business in the changing world.

Suddenly I had had an experience whereby in a very short time I had manipulated my emotions and my thoughts, bringing them from utter despair to a great high, with no medications except the ones that were prescribed to me for high blood pressure or fibromyalgia.

I quickly realised how easily our brains are affected by our own thoughts and intentions. Unexpectedly, I found that I had a message that was important to share with the world. So, just as happened thirty years ago when I went around the world talking about pornography, I found that I was putting myself out there on a platter and sharing my experiences.

I am again convinced that there is a positive angle in everything. Once more I can see the connections. It is humbling, and it is so clear. I have truly experienced that everything is energy and that when you redirect the energy, through changing your intention, everything changes.

CHAPTER 3

The World through My Eyes

> When you eventually see through the veils to how things really are, you will keep saying again and again, this is certainly not like we thought it was.
>
> —Rumi[1]

Some time ago I attended an Unstoppable Women[2] event in Brisbane, where there was a discussion about when people had felt the most powerful and most at the top of their world. In other words, at what point in time did people think that we had it all? This prompted me to think about my online affair, or scam, from a new point of view, namely, how things were seen and experienced thirty years ago when there was no Internet, compared to how we see them now in the digital age.

This chapter is designed to help the reader understand where I come from in relation to world issues and so contribute to an understanding of the underlying issues that are really at stake in the world today.

Here I am wondering how much the world does really change in thirty years. Or is it better to wonder how much it is our own way of looking at things that matures or changes? My wondering is based on the belief that during the last thirty years we seemed to have moved light years forward in the use of technology and our understanding of human behaviour. We have also encountered many new challenges, such as global warming and global networking in cyberspace, in real time. How are we to understand the ever-expanding human consciousness that is taking us to new heights?

Let's see how I remember it. In the summer of the Northern hemisphere of 1982, I was living in Sweden with my two young kids and my husband. We had bought my great-grandmother's old house in Finland and dreamed of living in the country after graduating from university. It was the Scandinavian dream come true. That summer there were two events that now, when I think about it, define my world as I saw it then, through the rose-coloured glasses I am sure I had on.

There was an international Peace Conference in Ahvenanmaa, Finland, with many of the top women's peace movement representatives from around the world. In that conference I was representing Sweden. The second event was the Women's Peace March from Helsinki to Moscow. More than ten thousand people were gathered to start at the old Kirkkonummi Church front steps. I had composed the marching song for the march. I sang it from the steps and then continued to sing for the next ten kilometres, to Helsinki Parliament House, where there were even more people joining in.

In my mind, the summer of 1982 stands as more idyllic than all the years before or after. That summer, I felt I had it all and that the world was a better place because of all the efforts women were making. I was young, I admit—only twenty-five—but somehow my research topics, despite all the troubling issues that I had already investigated, had not really made it to my consciousness deeply enough to affect me personally. I was confident in my belief in a more righteous world through the efforts people were putting into making it happen.

During the conference I would walk through the tranquil Ahvenanmaa landscape with Ninel, who was one of the leaders of the USSR (Russian) women's peace movement. She was so well trusted by the regime of the time that she could travel to Finland without an aide or anyone from the USSR side controlling her actions. I would tease her because her name was that of her great hero, Lenin, spelled backwards. We would also have conversations about Karl Marx and about her conviction that the man could do no wrong. I would keep finding flaws in his behaviour and his thinking, and in the end I got her to admit that he was wrong in not recognising his daughter, Eleanor. Ninel was so good-humoured about it though.

The second person I walked with was the American representative, Wilma, then the leader of the American feminist movement. She was such a lovely person. We got to be really close; she said that she would adopt me, and she encouraged me to translate my research on pornography into English for the entire world to see. And then there was Hilkka, from Finland, who was with the United Nations. She told me that I "was a kind of person who could do anything, when all the others only could do what they could."

Singing from the steps of the Kirkkonummi Church at the beginning of the Women's Peace March must have been one of the highlights of my life. I remember it so well! All the hope, all the goodwill, and all the conviction focused on that one moment in time. And suddenly the world was better for that one moment in time.

Even four years later—standing in Anaheim, California, holding hands with all the people who had joined hands for world peace across the continent, from one ocean to another through the USA—I was hopeful. Despite having researched pornography and violence against women in war for the four previous years, I had not felt a deep understanding of the consequences that knowledge brought. It had still not hit my person. My life was at the top of the pyramid.

I was pregnant with my third child, in love with my husband, conversing with all the leaders of the feminist movement in the world, I had just had a drumming session with one of my most my favorite authors Starhawk, had toured the USA to talk about pornography in different women's studies centres in several universities; had a newly released and signed copy of *The Creation of Patriarchy*, from Gerda Lerner; and I was holding hands with my wonderful friend Gloria. Here too, one moment was proof of the better world we were all contributing to.

I never would see Ninel or Wilma again, though I did make it to the memorial remembrance session for Wilma at the Iowa Women's Conference in 1986. However, I did get to sit on the lecture series on United Nations at the Helsinki University, where Hilkka was in 1994, and I was able to join Gloria in Adelaide, Australia, in 1997 for the Fourth International Interdisciplinary Conference for Women. Every one of these moments was a defining moment for the betterment of the world. And then the digital age was upon us.

My 1980s were filled with love, hope, romance, babies, action, fun, and deep engagement. My 1990s were filled with love, service, reflection, caring, and deep concern. My 2000s were filled with awe, love, loss, understanding, and deep caring for the world and the community around us. Finally, my 2010s have been filled with love, caring, loss, apprehension, and deep anxiety for the world.

My own yearning for romance was satisfied by research into romance books and popular culture as well as by following the trends that emphasised the deep concerns that I had in my previous life as a researcher. I guess that the Internet romance or affair was a wake-up call for me to re-examine the world as I saw it, and this book is the result of that reflection.

In 2010 I joined Facebook, and social media started to make sense to me. I got reacquainted with my old childhood and feminist friends, not only online but by actually visiting them around the world. I got rid of my inhibitions about online banking and now move money around online with the best of them. I pay my bills online, and instead of cash I move money between accounts for services required. It is the new digital world. I love my iPad and iPhone and can't imagine a day without them. In fact, when recently I had a day without, I felt lost and had clear withdrawal syndromes.

Many people I know have found love online. In fact, somewhere I read that every fifth marriage is formed through online meetings. Can that really be true? My son found the mother of his child online, and two of my dearest friends found their loving husbands there. If I think about it, why wouldn't I try as well? There is nothing to lose in trying, right? Except maybe money through scamming—but whoever told you about that? Not many warnings there, were there?

My 2014 was filled with the short-lived two months' Internet romance/scam experience, as this hit me hard. I could say that maybe it was not so much because I lost money but rather because I had to manage the deep loss of my idealistic beliefs about romance. I had to redefine the world I live in and again face the deep realities that I now see around me—and that is not on the outside.

On the outside, I see a beautiful home, a magnificent view, and lots of caring and loving kindness around me through my family and friends. Inside, I feel deep sorrow for the world we live in.

I am reading a book. It is called *Fury*, and it consists of women writing about the violence they have encountered.[3] It is Australian, and I come from Scandinavia. At least now one would expect that the world would be a decent place for women, children, and the underprivileged to live in, but it is not.

I am going to the movies. As I write this chapter, the movie *Fifty Shades of Grey* has just came out, so I am going to see it and review it for our fraud prevention group. This is a controversial movie, wherein bondage is normalised to the general public. It is an example of how something that thirty years ago would have been seen in Copenhagen only in the Green Light District has now been depicted as normal, for mainstream people. Of course, the movie is a watered-down version of the book that has been the most successful romance book series of the decade. I wonder what that says about us, right now.

I am watching TV. There's been three hours on *You* about wedding dresses and wedding planning. People are desperately seeking love and romance. It really makes you want to try on a dress yourself. The *You Channel* programs range from the one depicting life at the edge of Alaska, where people hunt bears to survive the winter (so for me it is very nostalgic), through to the other extreme. That includes programs where women and men are organising the one event that defines what is often the most romantic moment of their lives—their wedding day— and they are paying a fortune for it.

I am following YouTube. I am really immersed in the lives of Pewdiepie and Cutiepiemarzia. They met through networking online and are the epitome of a romantic young couple of the digital age. I see a boy and a girl, but I also see trends that I feel deep concern about. They are soft spoken, fun-loving and cute, Swedish and Italian.

I am also following what children see, from the wholesome Holderness family fun depicting a loving domestic atmosphere through songs to the other extreme where adults open toys, mostly pink, and play with them online for young children like my own granddaughter to watch. I see a lot of princess parties. Pink, pink. I love Sofia Grace and her pink-coloured world, which was improved by Ellen DeGeneres when she discovered Sofia Grace and her cousin Rose and took them under her wing. It is all so commercial and fun. But Sofia Grace is enjoying it like crazy.

I am following Facebook, what is put there by my friends and the authors I follow—ideas, organisations, and whatever. I read romance books that are full of violence and something I would call despair. They are mostly about vampires and shifters. I might be wrong, as I have read some really good reality-based stories as well, but I am used to following trends. I read a lot about wars, oppression, and sharia courts. I read about children being molested, as this exists in the structures of our society. I read about nine-year-olds and younger being married off to men older than their grandfathers. I read about it happening in Australia. My country. Where has the romance gone?

I am a historian by education. I see the long perspective. The last two to four thousand years of history are laid out in front of me. Up to now, it doesn't look as if we have learned anything much about being civilised, caring, inclusive, and kind to one another. I see that the top 1 per cent has owned the world and that through the ages those in the middle percentiles can have expected a live a fulfilling life—but in a short while it has changed. Despite governments wanting restriction, the digital age has brought everything to everyone's perusal, all around the world—every little indecency we were not aware of or could have been unaware of before. How are we coping with that? And how does my brief online scam bring this to the forefront for me to reflect on? It is as they say on YouTube: My name is Elina. This is my life. Thank you for watching!

What are we to make of all this?

The new world has everyone in its grip. It is an immediate Instagram, YouTube, Facebook, Twitter, and whatever-anyone-prefers world. What thirty years ago was an experience for only those present is now instantly broadcast throughout the world for all to experience as a secondary observer from every possible phone. The dribble effects are seen far and wide on the social media, whereas previously the only report would have come to us through the daily papers, if indeed it was reported. I am contemplating whether what we can see happening today is the depth of the experience or the width of the experience. Certainly everyone has his or her own personal angle to report. I am now able to write this book and self-publish it throughout the world, whereas previously I would have been limited by locality and by language as well.

In a world like this, it is easy to get lost in the information overflow and easy to get scammed in the belief that people are honest in their reports, even if you are well educated and alert.

I am reading a book about one Internet scam; it's based on the true story of a woman with the pseudonym of Christina who came to talk to us at one of the fraud prevention group meetings in Brisbane. The book is called *The Transformation of Love*,[4] and I am wondering how my understanding of love has changed and transformed during the last thirty years.

CHAPTER 4

How are the Sex, Romance Book reading, and Pornography Industries Connected with the Romance Scams Industry?

One of the most startling books I ever read was called *Dreaming the Dark*. The book was written by Starhawk and was published in the early 1980s. Her statement about what society is has haunted my mind ever since. She wrote that society is not static but instead is a system and sometimes "qualitatively different from…the sum of its parts."[1] These words were written in connection with the history of the witch hunts during the fifteenth to seventeenth centuries. The words are effective, and the more I think about them, the more connections I find that validate what she wrote about pornography, history, and violence. In relation to my own experience with romance scams, it is now more important than ever that we should look into what it is in our society that sets the rules regarding people's behaviour towards each other. Will we get the right answers if we ask the right questions?

Here are my questions: How is it that we come to understand the world we live in? How do we cope when something terrible happens and we have to understand it and deal with it? How can we possibly recover? Of course people do it differently. There are as many ways as there are individual persons coping with drama or trauma; however, we each define our own situation.

In January 1982 I attended the First International Interdisciplinary Congress on Women in Haifa, Israel. I was a very young university student and had not even finished my degree. At the time, I had changed from languages and literature studies to social studies at the University of Umeå in Sweden. However, I had previously had the privilege of being invited to become one of the founding members of the Kvinnoforskningseminariet, the women's studies group at my university. By traveling to Haifa, I was following the advice of a seasoned feminist who had told me that going to conferences would surely be the quickest way to find out what was going on in the world. It became my way to keep ahead of what were the best trends to research.

So I sat in the congress, listening to woman after woman—and a few men—talking about the situation of women in the world, from their own perspectives. On the last day, some American women spoke about pornography and violence. I was shocked by the information and felt that I had to investigate it. I was from Sweden and certain that the presented data would not be accurate for Scandinavia. But in three short months of research, I found that it was. And so began my career in researching sexuality from every angle possible.

I was fortunate to be invited to travel extensively around the world to talk about this subject. Some of my work was published, and some was not. It was a huge learning curve. My research progressed from the study of pornography from the sociological, pedagogical, and literary angles to studying violence against women in war. At that point I was done.

One of my first literary research projects was uncovering the general plot line in the Mills & Boon romance novels during the early 1980s. In order to make the statistics as simple as possible, I read exactly one hundred randomly selected books translated into Swedish. It turned out that the plot line was always the same, with not much deviation. There would be a man of around thirty years of age and a much younger woman, who had just turned twenty and was preferably a virgin. There was no sex before marriage—hardly any sex at all—but plenty of kissing. I still remember the first book I read in English that had a graphic sex scene in it. It was written by Sandra Brown; it was one of her early books. I still own that particular book.

The aim of these books during the early period was to create sexual tension. For an author, it was all about finding creative ways to arouse the reader with hints of sexual tension rather than descriptive scenes. Since my first experience with reading graphic sex scenes in romance novels, the industry has progressed from one trend to another in terms of what is a popular theme that could catch the reader's interest. Over the same period of time, the sex scenes have become more and more graphic. It has become soft porn for women, which might be as addictive as online porn for men.[2]

I have been able to follow these trends from the historical through to contemporary themes, then fantasy, and then to suspense and through time travel to sci-fi fantasy, with variations in between. More recently it has been the vampires and the shifters that have become really popular. The latest trend has been the normalisation of sadomasochism as standard sexual behaviour. And still the information I got at Haifa in 1982 hounds me. Here are the notes I recorded:

- 50% of men become excited by the pictures they see.
- 51% of men say that they could rape a woman if they would not get caught.
- Ed Donnerstein's early research shows that when men are shown movies where there is violence without sex, men prefer to choose women as their victims in the outburst of violence.
- 72% of Playboy's readers believe that women want to be raped.[3]
- Research shows that children replicate what they see around them.

In addition to this, I soon discovered the following:

- Early Swedish research showed that what young people thought about sex correlated well with what they read.[4]
- If everything that is stated here can be argued against, then a Norwegian researcher Anja Meulenbelt has proof that pornography points to a victim for the violence, namely women.[5]

These figures have bothered me for the last thirty years. Luckily, time is a great solver of problems, and if we examine the latest in academic research into this subject—which we will do—we can find that it has now been proved beyond doubt that we are affected by what we see in our world.

In my sociology classes at the university, I was introduced to many theories about how to look at and understand the world we live in. Of all these, I have found one theorist in particular who continues to help make sense of the world. So useful is this contribution that I can imagine how almost anything in the world would become clearer through the eyes of one of the most famous economists of the early twentieth century, namely Thorstein Veblen.

Through his eyes I imagined the rise of the women's movement and the leisure class, and it struck me as so fitting that the women who had time on their hands would be the ones who would come up with demands for better conditions for themselves and other underprivileged people—once they had time to think about other things beside birthing babies and toiling under hard labour.

So let's put my hypothesis to the test. Let's find connections and, finally, a common denominator between the subjects of pornography, romance books, and romance scams. We will use Thorstein Veblen's classical theories of economy, compiled from his two most famous books, *The Theory of the Leisure Class* (1899) and *The Theory of Business Enterprise* (1904)[6] as our very own and much-simplified pattern for the development of "conspicuous consumptions." I always picture in my mind's eye a funnel in 3D, where anything of interest can be dropped in and the common denominator will emerge from the other end.

Basically, his theory states that consumption of goods follows a pattern, going from the privileged population to the general population, from the rich few to the masses, from the general to specialisation and then to consumerisation, and that the catalyst is the possibility of leisure time over working time. According to his theory, women in our society are raised and educated to consume, and men are raised and educated to provide. We are not talking only about our present era. This division and distinction has been long in the making. We can start from classical times, when writing was in the form of poems, both erotic and adventurous. In Greece a special class of harlots named *porne* was formed, with special orders to entertain the trading merchants of Athens. The word pornography comes from the Greek word *pornographos,* meaning the writings describing the "porne" and their customers. The modern definition of the word pornography follows suit in the form of writings, pictures, and expressions of behaviour that will sexually arouse audiences.

In classical times, the romance scam was performed through warfare, as it was a custom that the conquering side would kill or maim the men of the losing side and capture their women for servitude, sexual and otherwise. The women would eventually have to change their support to the fathers of the children who were conceived if they wanted to look out for their welfare. It is notable that in our era this is a worldwide phenomenon.[7]

The next big watershed in the funnel was the invention of the printing press. In the writing genre, book printing would enable the rise of the novel—first to the educated and eventually, as time passed and the opportunity emerged, to the masses and to women in the form of romance novels.

In the pornography field, the printing of pictures, graphic books, and cards flourished. Combined with the rapid rise of literacy, this enabled a much larger population to enjoy books. For those who could not access books, the rising advertising industry solved the problem through pictures. It was noticeable that, at the same time, the thirst for sex became more and more fervent so that in one century, by the Victorian era, there were over fifty pornography shops in London alone. In addition, the evolving interest in archaeology enabled affluent people to collect a wide range of Greek and Roman reliefs and other erotica that had been discovered in the new digs.

The printing press also enabled the recording of the memoirs of the great Casanovas who scammed women and, of course, made widespread use of women as bait for money in the brothels.

The publishing houses prospered, and the emerging film industry ensured the popularisation of the most successful books and scripts, including the pornographic.

In the scamming industry, the newfound ease of the international postal and banking services would greatly help perpetrators. This would eventually get even easier thanks to the introduction of computers as tools. Technology would soon render obsolete the typewriter, and keeping track of people would improve with the newly invented memory chip. Where we are now, technology continues to get cheaper and memory capacity continues to double every eight months. This enables more and more people to log online and contribute to the ever-widening network with its ever-increasing possibilities for fraud.

The 1980s brought about a great diversification of the women's romance-book industry and the establishment of feminist research as a mainstream research genre at universities. Meanwhile, the popularisation of sci-fi as a mainstream option in the movies, plus the mainstreaming of documentaries about pornography, would enable the world to also start treating popular culture as a worthy discussion genre. And then came the Internet. With it there emerged a totally new mindset for looking at the world. In some ways, that was then and this is now—and yet all that was still remains.

So now we have digital books and publishing, digital cameras and movie production, email, social media, and the Internet dating scene. Everything is individualised. Anyone can write a book and publish it, anyone can publish a porn video on the net, and anyone can upload a fake profile on dating sites—or anywhere else on social media sites, for that matter. And they do! Not only production but also consumption is both digital and immediate, through home computers, tablets, apps, and digital downloading. What is most interesting is that it is free. According to their own discretion, people do download what is freely available online, from descriptive porn to the graphic romance and other books. In Western culture, the changing attitudes towards what is considered the right behaviour get downloaded as well, through the thousands of international TV pay channels enforcing the Hollywood definitions of right and wrong.

Meanwhile, behind the scenes, there has been over thirty years of unravelling how to read our DNA print. The Human Genome Project[8] was completed in 2003, and since then just about everything related to our way of looking at the world has been rapidly changing. The very idea of a person being able to change his or her own gene expression has freed the world from being stuck to one's own genetics and culture. The new medical technologies enable our very brains to be examined to ascertain how we function. In fact, we have finally found a common denominator for just about everything, and that is the brain. One of the interesting findings has been that the brain does not differentiate between what occurs as real to us and that which is from the imagination. This new understanding is crucial.

If we want to find a common denominator for romance books, pornography, and romance scamming, then we find it in the manipulation of our emotions with images to arouse us and make us want more of the same. In the context of pornography, scamming, and romance book writing, this manipulation is to persuade us to spend money. What happens in our bodies while we engage in reading romance books or perusing pornographic materials? For a victim of scamming, this is equivalent to a state of vulnerability and can be compared to addiction. It then becomes a question of how to deal with the overflow of hormones to the brain.

CHAPTER 5

How to Recognise Your Belief System

There is a story about Mara, the god of ignorance, in Buddhist thought. Once Mara and his attendant were walking on the road, when they saw a man meditating. The man was looking very happy as he focused on the ground before him. The assistant asked Mara what the man had found.

"A piece of Truth," said Mara.

Later, the assistant asked Mara whether it did not bother him that people kept finding pieces of Truth.

"Not at all," said Mara. "Usually it is only a matter of moments before they will make a belief out of it."

To put it in modern psychological context, consider this: "One of the central contentions of social psychology from the 1950s to the present has been that people justify themselves, their associates, and the world around them, in the sense that they use ideas to provide validation and legitimacy to all these things."[1]

How open are we to new ideas and new experiences, without bias? How often do we use our own restrictions to cement the status quo in our lives because we do not like change? And why on earth am I writing a chapter on this issue in a book focused on describing and recovering from romance scams? These were some of the questions I wanted answered for myself.

While undertaking research into romance scams, I have come across many discussions about why it is that scammers—especially those from Africa or from some other so-called developing-world countries—find it justifiable to scam people of the so-called developed. Some online conversations with the scammers have actually revealed that they feel their behaviour is justified because the women they scam are "rich bitches" who can afford the money. Where do these kinds of beliefs come from?

T. G. Diamond's book, *My Darling Davis: How Real is Your Love?*[2] really struck a chord with me, and I can relate to her scamming experience, although mine was not nearly so complicated. In her book she talks about how hard it was to let go of the relationship with the scammers because it had been such an emotional high. In closing my affair, I also sent a note to my scammer, telling him how much I had loved his attention and that I did not regret the feelings he had aroused in me but I *did* regret that it was not really true. Letting go is very frustrating and getting to understand you own biases about the world around you is even harder. Let's look at some ways of doing this, to see if we can recognise some common stereotypes.

We think we are knowledgeable about the world, and yet we might be surprised to know that we are largely ignorant of the real facts that lie behind our belief systems. We accept as fact the assumptions we have learned at school or inherited from our families. Yet these ideas have been delegated to us by people who themselves were perhaps relying on outdated facts and figures. Thus we are relying on a biased world view in order to validate our own behaviour. This is called system justification.[3] Its aim is to preserve the status quo. It is based on the understanding that our brain gathers information and forms patterns from them. It is easier for us to stay within what we have learned than to apply new knowledge and change these patterns.

However, change is inevitable. Take the mobile phone, for example. How many years ago was it that we did not have such gadgets? Not so long ago—yet can we even imagine back to that time when we didn't have them? Certainly people in their twenties could not, as mobile phones have been part of their reality since birth. Our memories work through pattern-building. And the most memorable moments to us are those that stand out from the continuum.

So, what we are accustomed to doing, when all else fails, is stereotyping our world into dualities. Such dualities allow us to preserve the information that validates whatever it is that we consider most useful to us in a given situation. One such set of contrasts is that of rich and poor, the affluent world and the Third World. In addition, of course, we already live in the duality of a masculine-biased world, where women are thought of as the *other*. The concept of the other can be easily projected onwards to other suitable parties, such as enemies at war. It is a built-in pattern within the structures of our society.

Let's consider the stereotyping of our world into poor countries and rich countries and the associated belief that the rich countries and their populations are able to aid the poor countries. In fact, if we look closely at world statistics, we find that since 1975 the world has changed considerably, and such a division does not exist any more. We just had not kept up with the new data.

Given the current rate at which we are producing information, it might be hard to realise that most of it is outdated at just about the moment when it is presented to the world. The implications are considerable; this means that most educational materials, for example, are based on outdated data. Not even the media that often guide our world view seem to have done their homework well enough to alert us to these changed circumstances regarding factual information.

Ola Rosling, CEO of the Gapminder organisation in Sweden and founder of the Ignorance Project, will have you convinced in no time at all that supposed facts are all based on a mixture of personal bias, outdated facts, and media bias. Furthermore, he asserts that "screwed information," combined with our "intuition" leads to a largely biased world view that in turn enables us to validate whatever we *want* to see as accurate.[4]

The world according to pornography is based on the world view that women are the "other" gender. That gender is supposed to always be available and to serve as a possession to provide sexual service and produce children in the world. This has been the common view of everyone, including women, in this masculine "power-over" society presented to us through the writings of many men of ideas, from

Plato[5] to Rousseau.[6] This view reflects the masculine power-over patterns built into our society.

Western culture might give women more freedom, but looking at it from the bigger picture, we have a lot to accomplish in order to close the gender gap. This bias lends a fundamental pattern to any other world view. In the world of scammers, for example, the stereotyping comes from the belief that there are two worlds, the rich and the poor, and the rich can be scammed into aiding the poor, because they can afford it. Every country has a widening gap between the poor and the rich, which provides the scammer with the possibility of validating his or her belief that scamming is justified as good business and is a valid job description. For example, in Australia, who would be able to comprehend that in India there are more billionaires than among the whole population of Australia—while, in our minds, the country is preserved as a developing country?

The world view of "the other" is very much supported by the stereotyping patterns learned through guerrilla war. In the context of this world view, women are treated as tools to aggravate the enemy side, because women are looked upon purely as possessions. Any regular watching of world news and affairs will confirm this. Both sides train their solders into believing that the enemy is the disposable, non-existent other. This then validates their existing strategies for conquering the enemy territory.

My research into war practices focused on the Palestinian war during the 1980s. The updated information on the situation between Israel and Gaza reveals that the cultural customisation continues for generations and is very hard to overcome; there is always something happening to validate the situation on both sides. My personal experience of such cultural customisation comes through the generational discord between Russia and Finland.

My memory of the situation there had been boosted by the memories of my Finnish ancestors and their suspicion and decisions about how to act towards Russia from the Finnish side. I find that I can easily take sides according to that amplified history if I am not careful with my thoughts. For example, I can "see" my own great-grandfather hiding for days underneath a house in Helsinki when Governor General Bobrikov was murdered in 1904[7] without ever thinking that I was only born in 1956 and could not possibly understand the situation my great-grandfather was in at the time. I cannot even remember in which context this information was whispered to me by my grand-aunt, as I was so young, but there it is, a shocking fact placed in my memory. I cannot any more even verify whether what I was told is true or from her imagination. Everyone connected has long ago passed away. And just as in many other historical Finnish family albums, the assassin Eugen Schauman's[8] photograph can be found in my family's album. During the early twentieth century, Schauman was viewed as a great hero in Finland, despite or because of what he did. Tacitly, his action cemented the belief system that became the basis on which decisions were being made during the following world wars in Finland.

Ethical conversations about the world and what is the right action to take are always complicated. The General Assembly of the United Nations gives definite proof as to how biased our world views can be and how short the memory is when world politics and biases define the right action to take in order to work together for the betterment of the Earth's population as the whole.

The world of romance books reflects and mirrors these biases at every stage, from definitions of the book genres right through to the biological preference in character building to arouse the audience and persuade them to buy more of the same. It is a great money business, as is the world of pornography and scamming. It is all focused towards wiring the brain's rewards system. And thanks to the brain research that continues to inform and amaze us, we can now much better determine what the chemistry of love, sex, and money is.

CHAPTER 6

What to Know about the Chemistry of Love and Arousal

It is interesting to reflect on what we know of love today in comparison to what we knew before we could put our heads in an electromagnetic scanner and literally see neural pathways connecting. We can now immediately determine what parts of the brain are activated and what chemicals are produced at any time during our progress from meeting the one we are falling for until the relationship either matures or breaks down.

Quite early in my online affair, I undertook a research project on two subjects. Firstly, I wanted to understand the neurochemistry of love and sex, and then I wanted to know what new articles or blog posts were available on how to maintain the relationship for as long as possible. I got millions of hits on Google, and weeding through the information overflow was most tedious but also very enlightening to me.

I was fascinated by one particular website, health-science-spirit.com, which focused on how to maintain love and the balance of chemicals in a relationship. My interest derived from a conversation about *tantra* and love I'd had with my online "friend," and I wanted to know what there was about it on the Internet.

I found Walter Last's research on natural therapies and health, and particularly on the neurochemistry of sex, very interesting. He concisely describes what happens to us when we fall in love. That is all we need for determining what is connected in our brain when we watch porn, or read romance and graphic novels—that is, those situations where we imagine relationships instead of experiencing them in real life. The second resource I would recommend for everyone interested in female psychology in relation to sex and biology is *Vagina: A New Biography*, by Naomi Wolf.[1] It is one of the most startling books and is sure to produce a reaction in anyone as well as give lots of useful information about women.

What I have learned from analysing my own experience with online romance and scams is that scammers rely on repeat performance, just as romance writers do. In the case of romance writing, the aim is to arouse and engage the audience with the characters and the plot, thus ensuring that the audience wants to buy the next book written by that author or the next book in the series. In the case of romance scamming, the aim is to make sure that the targets of scamming are hit with as much of the hormone dopamine as possible, to ensure they repeatedly fall under the scammer's spell, this ensuring continuous money flow. For the scammer, it pays to understand how to quickly get his subjects aroused and engaged. What is critical is to determine how to keep the subject's aural cortex (the lizard brain) focused or obsessed—and not her frontal cortex, which requires rational thinking. The small primal aural cortex part of their brains keeps victims fixated on the romance, floods their brains with dopamine, and prevents them from making decisions using their intellectual reasoning, which would be happening if they were using the frontal cortex.

The intensity that is created very quickly ensures that the victim anticipates good experiences now that their hormones are flowing. This helps to affirm that they are hooked on the affair. For the victim, it is an additional self-perpetuating trap when they keep rereading the messages, with the same hormone-spreading results. Sometimes the scammer also calls the victim and uses his voice to hook her/him even further.

This certainly happened in my case. The voice affected my nervous system directly and even eased the pain associated with my fibromyalgia. This made me even more vulnerable to the scammer, as I felt much better physically after the call.

Let's look at it from the point of view of the victim's ultimate satisfaction. That would be the equivalent of orgasm, with the high production of the chemical oxytocin in the brain. Here we tread a fine line, as the experience is often described as similar to consuming heroin. It takes around two weeks to really come down from a heroin high and just as long to come down from the experience of a full-blown orgasm, yet lesser levels of oxytocin, especially when sustained over time, can also be extremely satisfying. Those who talk about safe ways to maintain the longevity of relationships are now newly appreciating the wisdom of former gurus and others who maintained platonic love relationships while directing their emotions to reach heightened states of enlightenment. In this way, they could keep up the level of chemicals in their brains just by regulating oxytocin, the cuddle hormone.

What I found interesting is that women can regulate their oxytocin flow through clitoral orgasms, which really only serve their body health through stress release. This kind of orgasm is entirely separate from reproduction. Men do not rely on this, as their sperm produces enough of the hormone for them. Thus, those who can satisfy women's need for oxytocin in other ways than penetration are able to ensure their continued affection. And while they did not know about the brain and its functions at the time, the practices of the gurus, such as *tantra*, for example, accorded exactly with the kind that modern brain research might consider healthy in terms of the longevity of relationships. However, the predominance of information that concentrates on penetrative sex, combined with the overflow of pictures on this same topic in the digital world of the twenty-first century, provides a huge temptation to anyone to become aroused, attached, and addicted. This is as fertile a ground for scammers as it is for those who are looking for and finding heightened experiences.

The key to having a lot of positive and comforting experiences is arousal. In order to keep ourselves in an aroused state, we need to be engaged and inspired. Our brains do not necessarily make a distinction between what is real and what is imaginary. The brain releases dopamine, even though it only predicts that something will happen based on how it has been trained or according to the previous positive activity. And not only this, but our brains are wired to cognitively pay attention to what arouses us. Here lies the trap for both women and men.

Maybe the generalisation that women's and men's brains work in different ways is a bit too far-fetched but certainly we are socialised in very different ways and as a result out brains fire in a different way as well. Men are socialised to become more graphic and territorial. Women are socialised to become more involved in relationship-building and storytelling. Thus men are more affected by arousing pictures and women by arousing stories. Look at the most popular TV programs. They involve violence or abuse, warfare, physical or verbal conflicts, crime or general risk-taking, and sex. We all want an emotional rush— in slightly different ways. Understanding how to write a convincing story requires reading about how different stages of fear and satisfaction work on the brain. Knowing how to handle the sudden rush of hormones that invades our brains when we see an action film with high risk-taking or graphic sexual encounters is a very lucrative skill for a good screenwriter to have.

Pornography has similar effects on a man and more easily than on a woman, although the situation is changing with the online availability of videos and pictures. The worst cases of pornography addiction bring on isolation from real-life partners and result in solitary engagement, with the total focus that of watching porn and masturbating in front of it so that the hormones flood the brain.

Romance books are interesting too. We have seen that the sex scenarios in romance books have changed considerably. The stories are now much more graphic compared to, let's say, twenty years ago. Younger and younger readers are being aroused by what would have been adult situations only a few decades ago. On the other hand, the dichotomies between what is considered suitable and what is not are being much more defined as black or white. Many moral issues are being dominated and defined by Hollywood and a new American puritanism. Then again, the digital age has brought much more visibility to many issues that were well hidden thirty years ago, including cultural biases, incest, and paedophilia. At the same time, people are faced with plenty of alluring information, and once they surrender to the temptation, it is much harder these days to keep their actions under the radar than it was thirty years ago.

We are well into the age of competitiveness versus competence. Not only are the victims or targets for possible crimes and scamming savvier, but the scammers are more professional, and just as in their targets' brains, their own efforts also produce a steady rush of chemicals to their own brains. The act of training their victims to want more and more of the same is their particular skill, just as a skilled romance writers have their audience craving the next book. The undertones are quite similar, actually.

The scammers produce fictional profiles online, complete with characterisation and effortlessly flowing storylines. The pictures are often stolen from real people, usually from models or from socially authoritative figures. The scenarios are well rehearsed. It does not matter whether the scammer is alone or in a group, as the profile and the character can be built by many and also acted out in different media by many, all without the knowledge of the victim. In practice, one person could be writing a storyline, another Skyping, and yet another could be the voice on the phone. This is very often the case with Russian scams.[2] For the victim, the storyline appears as a continuous experience.

And because the story is online, as in the email inbox or as Skype texts, there is the possibility for the victim to read and reread the messages so that the intensity of the affair produces a steady flow of hormones in the victim's brain. This can easily create an obsession about the lover that leads to a level of vulnerability that is easily exploited.

Interestingly, I did not read any romance novels while my online scamming experience was going on. This particular observation was actually one of the central discussions that amused me and the scammer during the affair. In a similar vein, many romance book readers report going back to the same familiar book again and again. I, for example, have my favourite romance books, as does everyone else who reads such fiction, and I can read them repeatedly in order to produce the same emotional high of dopamine. What is interesting is that the reader's brain anticipates the comforting experience and produces that cuddle hormone again and again. This is a sure way to quickly experience satisfaction. While this can be good, it can also be seen as a vulnerability that can be abused. Skilled writers or storytellers, for example, can train their audiences to want to buy their particular books again. This is an important part of a productive and efficient marketing strategy.

The scammers have very similar aims. They want the victim to be hooked on them as the provider of the cuddle hormone, even if the victim has unearthed the scam. They do this by insinuating that they have really fallen for their victim. This can lead to really serious crimes that we hear about in the news and social media.

Let's go back to my favourite economist, Thorstein Veblen, and his theory on behaviour and consumption. Let us bring more threads together by considering the action of reading romance, watching porn, and loving the online romance circuit, and comparing these to overeating. We know that Western culture, in its eating habits, promotes obesity. We also know that the food industry is taking the so-called scientific pathway in proving to the consumer that one ingredient or another is either the core of the problem or the cure for overeating at any particular time. This debate has lasted well over thirty years, and there is no end in sight. Losing weight has become a central issue in the promotion of processed-food products as the solution to the ever- increasing demand for easier access and cheaper food options.[3]

Let's compare online relationships, social media, online porn sites, and digital romance book consumption to eating an easily digested, energy-dense diet high in sugar, fat, and salt. And don't even start me on the topic of alcohol consumption. What we find is that the more complex the stimulus, the more it hits our reward buttons. All possible industries, including the love industry, have found that through "supernormal stimuli" of greater variety, we consume more than we would in normal surroundings. It is all artificially created, along the same lines as all the different varieties of ice-cream, in our Disneyland of love consumption. And if you think that this is not connected, then just consider what science could say about what happens if our online lover sends us chocolates as an unexpected surprise. My contemplated conclusion of such an occurrence is that the brain is literally screwed, to put it bluntly, if we then eat the said chocolate. Namely, that ardently uplifting act will ensure that our brain's orbitofrontal cortex, which is involved in the cognitive processing of decision-making, enhanced with our emotions, will keep us obsessing on our online lover for a long time.

CHAPTER 7

How to Use the Theory of Turning Emotion to Money and Develop a Perfect Pitch for Love for Scamming, Romance, and Pornography Industry Business

Is there a theory in turning emotion into money? I was amazed to find out that yes, of course there is. This is how it happened to me:

In the midst of my flourishing online love affair, I had been getting suspicious about the integrity of my online "friend." In order to cross- reference the facts, I had sent his credentials to my son so that he could look into them without my friend's knowledge. Just as my son sent me the email stating that what I was involved with was, in fact, a Ghana scam, my "friend" called from Ghana—so yes, it did all fall together quite nicely.

My immediate reaction was to keep conversation going with my online friend in order to help the police if needed. And at the same time, my researcher brain kicked in, as it always does. I wanted to add value to my own experience, and I plotted how I would collect some more information in order to use it in a creative way. At that point, the book idea had not yet come to me. During that particular weekend, I had attended a networking conference in Sydney, and I now wanted to apply what I had heard there to my experience.

At that conference, a very successful network marketing professional talked about his method of becoming a "Type Five personality." That is healthy, wealthy, and having lots of free time to do what one wants. It turned out that he had been mentored by a person who had in turn been mentored by Napoleon Hill, the man who wrote the classic *Think and Grow Rich*.[1] From this mentoring relationship, the networking specialist was inspired to develop a very entrepreneurial and successful business. He introduced the audience to the famous "self-confidence formula" by Napoleon Hill. I, of course, immediately downloaded the whole book and read it.

I was surprised to find that half of the book is actually about how famous and successful rich artists and entrepreneurs were inspired by their muses to be the best that they could be. The book laid out a theory that the quickest and most successful way to grow rich would be to transmute the emotion of sexual passion into money. I went, "Wow! This is just amazing! I am going to have so much fun with this!" The whole point of romance scamming is to ensure that the emotional high of target victims keeps them hooked on the relationships so that they will easily part with their money, to the scammers benefit. I suggested to my online friend that we would do exactly that. We would experiment to see whether our mutual emotion could be transmuted to creativity and abundance. He of course said that yes, he would go all the way with that.

Immediately, I did what the book was suggesting, starting to develop the definite purpose plan and reciting the self-confidence formula as instructed, twice a day. According to Napoleon Hill, what really counts is the level of emotion one puts into convincing the subconscious to start making the changes in one's situation—and then acting on this. The stronger the emotions, the better for manifesting your new life. This introduced me to a huge not-previously-known world of online webinars on abundance building and another series on meditation practices using what is called the Brainwave Entertainment.

Two weeks into this process, we had considered a great number of approaches for transmuting emotion into money. That is the scammers' business in a nutshell. That is when my online friend called me and asked if I had read *The Lazy Man's Way to Riches*, by Richard G Nixon.[2] Well, I had not, but I immediately downloaded the original Joe Karbo 1973 version and read it.[3] Again, it was fascinating to me that my friend related this late advertising guru to our experiment. The book directly communicates how to write persuasive texts that will ensure the sale of the product which, in the scammer's case, is love online.

Joe Karbo became a billionaire by selling his book through "direct response" marketing, writing ads in large newspapers and magazines around the world and sending the books to customers directly from his own office. He had a great talent for writing advertisements. These continue to be studied, and the methods he used are being taught in advertising and business schools at universities around the world. What startled me was his approach to writing an advertisement. He described it through a love letter to his wife.

So, here we have two great authorities, both testifying that strong emotions of love and sex make us tick and can convince us to do whatever the intention is behind the persuasion. Not only that, but both are suggesting practical methods that are used in many ways by people all over the world both for positive and negative intentions. Furthermore, both of these authorities had written their books long before the digital time, before the human genome project was even started, and before brain scans could show in detail what happens in the brain when the inducement is success. Yet their methods are very detailed.

Joe Karbo suggested that a successful and effective ad would need to be like a love letter focused on getting the right message through to the right audience. He laid out a few universal principles that apply to writing both a good love letter and an advertisement:

- Use the name of the person to whom the letter is directed,
- Tell the person how important he/she is as a user of the product,
- Make a valid promise that will insinuate the advantages and disadvantages of the product,
- And reassure that the product will work.

There also had to be a call for action, such as asking the target audience to buy the product.

Interestingly, when I examined the last message I ever received from my online friend, I found all these elements right there:

Dear Elina,
I want to say thank you so much for the lovely email and pictures you keep sending me. I really appreciate them as they make my day brighter. It was great talking to you on the phone, you take my breath away Elina. I really enjoyed hearing your voice so loud and clear and can't wait to hear it again soon. I am glad that you also have such strong feelings for me Elina because I wouldn't know what I would have done if I was the only one feeling this way. I give you my word I am going to always love and care for you, treat you with respect and make you happy always because you mean the world to me now ...[4]

To receive and read a letter like this would most probably flood your brain with dopamine, giving you that fuzzy feeling of great euphoria, which was the intention. The sad part is that this method can be used both when writing about real emotion of love for the receiver and to persuade your brain to produce the dopamine required to form attachment to a product being sold through an advertisement. The difference lies in the intention. In this case, the product is love. Once the attachment is formed, it can relatively easily be used to manipulate the target into parting from money or giving the services required.

In the online connection there is created a false intimacy between the scammer and the victim. This is reinforced with the use of well-rehearsed words taken directly from the world of advertising, direct contact achieved by chatting on Skype and texting on the phone, and an intimacy sealed by phone calls and voice reassurance. This is further reinforced by the feeling of unconditional acceptance that the scammer has created through a kind of Rogerian Therapy approach, whereby the scammer completely empathises with the target's personality traits and preferences.

This produces in the victim a heightened sense of belonging and emotion, one that is much more real than one finds when reading romance books. Here there is a real person who promises real human contact. This gets the hormones flowing and produces a sharpened tunnel view in the mind of the victim. This can lead to compulsive behaviours that modify decision-making due to intense, sharp-minded concentration focused on the Internet affair with the online "lover."

After successfully getting the target to focus only on the lover, the scammer as lover has an easy time turning the conversation around and asking for money. It feels like a natural aspect of an ongoing relationship that has been there for a long time already, despite the fact that it has only been a short while.

We are not taking into consideration here whether the practice of persuasion is ethically sound, even though both of the cited authorities used half of their books to encourage their audience to use highly ethical behaviour that would benefit everyone concerned and ensure the best possible results. Most of the webinars I have listened to on wealth-building take great care in emphasising to the audience the worth of helping others. The network-marketing business is all about helping others, and call centres are full of people giving friendly advice that is not meant to disturb people even when the calls are made right at dinner time. The intention is for good—however, at what point do we cross the line? When is it hurtful and destructive?

The theory of pornography persuades the user or the audience to believe that women, or whoever is objectified at the time, are disposable and changeable products that are manufactured and monetised for the use of those who can afford them. The message behind seeing everything in dual terms extends this theory into allowing the producer to justify the action by stereotyping the objects into whatever category is useful for gaining the intended results. In this case, the intended gain is money or services.

The romance-book industry works on the same principles by attempting to arouse the audience so they will buy and use more products, which in this case are books. So, too, does the porn industry, by producing more pictures, books, and graphic details online to generate addiction and, through it, the craving for more of the same for the audience and money the part of those who are benefiting. Finally, the scamming industry uses every way possible to direct the emotions of targets to automatic action in order to part them from their money.

This is a vicious circle, one in which the victims have to come up with their own methods of recovery. There seems to be not much available in the system that would support individual action to regain peace of mind or money they may have already lost in the process. As I thought about how I would get over my experience and make it worth something, I decided to write my own best-possible romance, based on my experience, for my own pleasure, just as I had always wanted.

CHAPTER 8

Why are Mature People More Vulnerable to Scamming?

When writing this book, I had just turned fifty-eight, which made me a *ripe-age* person. While talking about online dating, I've often heard that mature people are more vulnerable to romance scams. However, I have found no real evidence of that. They are certainly targeted more on the basis of this belief. The reasons are many, but still the question remains valid. Why does it appear that mature-aged people are the most vulnerable targets for romance scammers?

This question, of course comes, from my own experience as I try to understand why I became a target. Clearly, being of mature age was part of it.

We can start by identifying which age groups read the most romance books. It is not, in fact, older people but mothers aged between thirty- five and forty-five who comprise the largest reader group. Somewhere on the Internet I found data to identify who read the controversial book *Fifty Shades of Grey* and that was the result: highly stressed mothers who wanted a quick fix from the complexities of family life and child-rearing. The statistics I found on the net from 2012 also identified that less than 30 per cent of the readers had children, 14 per cent were over fifty-five, and 16 per cent were men. But those who are the most targeted victims for scammers are older—why?

There is no real profile for a person who falls for an online romance scam; however, there are some assumptions about what kind of people are likely to be online looking for new relationships, friendships, and possibly love. These people include those who are isolated, lonely, or thrill seekers and those otherwise not able or willing to engage themselves in the regular face-to-face dating scene. This would be the case for a lot of older women and men. For the purposes of statistics, those who are over fifty-five are counted as older people, and that includes the author of this book.

Mature people are actually also the most avid readers, and they mostly read for pleasure. This means that they read books regularly every day. Out of the full range of book genres available, romance books are being consumed with an ever-increasing lead. And if your count includes erotic romance books, the romance genre does take the lead from general fiction. In fact, I myself belong to that category of avid readers, yet during my online affair I did not have to read any romance books at all. I found it really striking that the online affair was able to maintain my full attention in such a way that I did not seek extra entertainment through books.

Contemporary romance books are mostly about new love, where the hero and the heroine are younger persons with less life experience or they are in their thirties with some experience but not lasting love. Books where the main characters are in their forties and over are scarce. There is a real void in romance books about older people's romantic stories. The reasons are many. In online discussions it is stated that it is not easy to write romance about mature people; this is because the authors must figure out what the characters did before the romance starts, and that might be quite tragic or boring. Who wants to read about that? So they say! Taking the evidence from the romance scam industry, we can see that this could be a large audience ready to explore new areas.

The romantic character stories that are the most successful—and that the scammers use in persuading their targets to part from their money—involve authoritative and successful, typically military men or business men, and beautiful model-like women looking for kind men of independent means. The most successful scammers are very professional communicators who are able to enhance the older generation's sense of freedom from their inhibitions and restrictions in everyday living. This was also so in my case.

After analysing the conversations I'd had with my own online friend, I came to identify two main points that most easily contributed to my falling for the scam: his rhetorical approach and his immediate reactions to my emails, chat conversations, and texts. We must keep in mind that everything in the scamming world is written as emails or as Skype chat and texts on the phone, so the conversations can be read by the target again and again for enjoyment and just for kicks. That is what I did.

Two approaches come to mind that help me understand why I fell for the scam. The first is provided by Deborah Tannen, who wrote about female/male communication. Her book *You Just Don't Understand: Women and Men in Conversation* was a revelation to me when it came out in 1990.

With her research on human communication, and especially the communication between men and women, Deborah Tannen highlights the fact that women and men react to and often understand words and expressions in different ways. When the understanding between partners conflicts, it can have far-reaching consequences for the relationship.[1] Connecting the dots here, where the intention is empathetic on both sides, and where people are willing to place themselves into one another's positions and work towards an unconditional positive outcome, the relationship can be sure to flourish, at least on paper. And that is where the online romance is situated, on paper and in the imaginary world—just as in romance books. This approach is quite literary. So why wouldn't an avid reader of romance equipped with aroused conditioning fall for a scam using this approach? I did

The second approach takes a stylistic perspective. I could detect from the discourse we were having that my scammer's conversations and reactions were distinctly constructed according to the principles of the famous psychologist Carl Rogers. Rogers, who invented Person- Centered Therapy, would have recommended as healing his approach which excelled in building understanding and empathy towards the conversation partner. I was greatly in need of therapy at the time.

Rogerian principles are about establishing similarity of outlook, unconditional positive regard towards the opponent, and emphatic understanding of the other's situation. Other heavy thinkers in this area have criticised this approach to therapy as a possible attempt to change the opponent's mind for the sake of mutually profitable cooperation. This could apply to the scammer's idea of working on getting what he wants from his targets by promising them whatever he feels they need the most. Carl Rogers predicted that as civilization becomes more refined and learned, kindness towards others will spread in the world. I would like that to be the true cause of action, but there is always the other side of the coin, which predicts that everything, even a seemingly good action, can be used to further a selfish agenda. It is all in the intention.

Consider this third factor in relation to the theory that mature people are more vulnerable for scammers. It is highly possible that with age some of our cognitive ability to doubt declines; this happens through the disruption of hormone balance in our brains. How many of us have heard stories about a mum, dad, or grandparent who believed the spam email promising them a million dollars to be true and genuine and went ahead and gave out their bank details and lost money on the scam. That was because they forgot to check with their children or grandchildren, who could have told them that it was a scam spam in the first place. Also, if anyone has ever been online looking for porn or registered for any porn site, they will have noted that the amount of spam in their email inbox increased considerably. That is the case for any kind of scams. How many of us older people know how to get rid of all that without assistance? If we can, we would be considered very computer savvy indeed. This medical-fact interpretation could be too far-fetched, but I must put it there to be considered in all fairness.

From my own experience I can say that being listened to and having an empathic ear, even through email and dating online, is a genuine turn-on or hook for a mature person. The storyline does not have to be really complicated as long as it genuinely enables us to feel we are being heard and deeply listened to. There is also the dimension of talking or writing to someone we do not see. This makes it easier to create quick attachment in the context that many older people have grown up trusting other people and their intentions. Being able to feel needed through empathetic action towards others reminds us, especially women, of the times when this was part of our lives, especially if we now live alone with no one to care for.

I told my phony friend about how I found it really mindboggling to think of him in a war zone at the same time that I was living peacefully in my own safe community; while he was in danger, I was safe. I told him how I was on my way to aqua aerobics and what was happening there. He answered that it would be a wonderful healing experience to come and join me at the pool in a country where people can be safe from harm. I would say that conversations like that would remind many older people of experiences they had shared with their own families. Many would know someone who has been at war and be able to relate. It would be an easy storyline to use to grow trust. Sensitivity in intimate questions would be an additional hook if the online "lover" could relate to the older person's sexual needs as well.

Relating to sexual issues seems to be a minefield for older people. There are so many beliefs and taboos that if someone were to be sensitive enough to listen deeply and react in an appropriate way, they would achieve certain success in getting the target to react in a positive way and in strengthening the trust they were building. I am sure that it would be true for the younger generation as well, but for the older generation, getting someone to believe that women or men in their fifties or sixties still could have an active sex life would be such a delight that they would probably say yes to parting with a few thousand dollars for that alone. Our culture is so attached to youth and looking young and fit that older people are easily left thinking that they are unable to love or be loved any more.

I am pretty much addicted to collecting movies about older people—that is, people over fifty. It is true that there are many more stories targeted towards the older generation than there were in the past. Forty years ago, when my great-grandmother was getting past her first century, longevity was a great accomplishment. Now the number of healthy centenarians grows every year. So maybe we should rethink this: What is the meaning of old?

CHAPTER 9

Scammers 101: Unveiled

This is the chapter of the book I have really been looking forward to writing, although to me it has seemed to be the hardest one to write. The original idea was to tell you what the scammers do and how they have acquired the skills to lure their targets into parting with their money. However, after further research and lots of discussions with other romance scam victims, I have decided to do it in a way that will be fun for me and, hopefully, also entertaining for the reader. I will put myself into the scammer's shoes. I will walk his path with unconditional understanding and empathy. I will tell you what I have learned by imagining myself as a scammer who was the best, with lots of professional skills. And judging from his attempts to scam me further, he was also very patient, imaginative, and well versed in several types of scamming. These ranged from identity fraud to financial fraud. I did like my scammer, Stephen's sophistication.

As a scammer, the first thing I need to do is to pick a country of origin. (My ethnicity needs to be Ghanan, as that is what the ethnicity of my scammer "friend" was.) As a person from Ghana, I am posing as a British/Australian major general in a peace keeping mission to Afghanistan. That is my main persona, but I also have others, including that of an American businessman from Texas. He is of Irish descent. I have downloaded nice pictures to match my characters and for each persona I have created a personal life story. In real life, I am under forty years old, black, a university graduate, 185 cm tall, in good health, and single.

I form part of a loose scammers' network that reaches as far as countries like Italy, Saudi Arabia and Indonesia. I use trusted friends in my circle. I speak several languages and am able to put on an Australian, British, or American accent. I am really good at research and have graduated from a good standing university in Ghana.

I started scamming mainly because I was not getting the good jobs I applied to. The competition for the jobs is stiff. There is still not much hope of my doing well, given the economic circumstances of my country. Besides, I want to live a high life. I think that I am better at scamming than most. In fact, I train others in this business. As a scammer, I earn up to $50,000 US per month. I have been in this occupation for nearly five years now and have a lot of experience. I do get high on my own success, but I am also careful. So, let me tell you a little bit about my background and how I convinced myself that scamming was the right profession for me in this world.

My country is one of the African countries with a rising economy and a blooming tourist industry. However, people with good education do not get jobs. We have to be inventive about it. More-developed countries send aid money to our country. They invest into this country only if it serves their own purpose. Nothing is free. Our part of the world is used to scamming its way to money from abroad. The system of scamming and fraud is inbuilt into the structures of our society despite it being condemned. You might have a good education, but it is easy to go with the flow, as scamming is very lucrative, although volatile.

I take pride in delivering the best of the best to my targets and keeping them on my radar long after they have figured out that it was a scam. I also take pride in my ability to be careful about my scamming and to reach my group's income goals. It is good to live the high life. We deserve it, and our targets in other countries can afford it. Being a scammer and rich makes me more attractive to girls who also like affluent lifestyle.

How does the scamming work?

I am part of a loose group of people who collaborate in scams around the world. The downside of it is that there is no real organisation behind it, and we need to acquire our own personal circle group for circulating money between countries. The plus is that these groups are so loose that we have an excellent ability to disappear when something threatens our security. It is also easy to hide from the police in an Internet café with the multicultural variety of people, including tourists. It does beat lying on the floor of small rooms full of young men working online. The other factor in our favour is that our set-up is not like the well-established mafia system of control and punishment. In our case it is free, entrepreneurial, and relatively easy to find your own feet. And you can stop whenever you want–if you can, that is.

I have a Batchelor of Arts in Business, with a marketing major. Through my work as a scammer, I have gained a lot of experience in what works best with regards to my targets in any situation. I give them what they ask for, and I get good monetary results for my group. I use all my knowledge in human psychology to find the vulnerabilities in my victims. Often I retain the contact with secondary scams after the first scam has been found out. My occupation is the online lover and as a lover I am the best. This world is full of fools for love. It is my market.

My hero is the Internet. It gives me all I need, including the information and the upskilling I am looking for. Google is gold. I learn sharpen my skills with every encounter with my targets. I never think about them as human beings, just as women or men I can manipulate to my will. Sometimes it is very entertaining. Sometimes the targets tell me so much–and so sincerely. I can keep them on their toes and enthral them like a vampire king. It makes me feel like the king of the world. I get my kicks from that, and the more forward the language, the better.

My aim is to build such report with my target that it results in the highest possible money exchange between us. Sometimes it can even be money laundering through the targets' bank accounts. Most often it is me creating storylines bringing forward the empathy of my targets and they will send me money. It can be thousands of dollars, if

I get the right kind of person. Mostly, I work on the social network. I build trust thorough emails, Skype, texting and phone calls.

I am particularly good at texting and sexting. You can imagine the kind of hook that texting several times a day creates in the mind of my target. And then calling them on the phone, particularly at night or early morning. The aim is to get the hormones their brain makes their body to produce flowing as high as possible. I send ready scripted and tweaked emails every day, with little notes of love, pictures and music. That is to say, I use all the available psychological methods to court my online love target.

The quicker the target has taken my bait, the quicker I can move to the next pace in the relationship. There I am free to ask my target to send me money for varying reasons – medical expenses for my family and me, flight tickets in order to meet them and even illegal papers to trick the international tolls. Everything depends on how responsive my target is to my charm. I am using the CamDecoy to monitor the messages beforehand, and tweak my responses accordingly.

I have attained a real British phone number online and use a voice changing device for my calls. Targets respond to low and sexy voice, most of the time. It is all simple brain chemistry. I ask the victims to send me money through the Western Union, MoneyGram or even by buying iTune cards. It is much harder to follow the money exchange there.

I always ask my victim not to discuss our relationship with other people, including the members of their extended family. This is to ensure that nothing comes between us. This approach works very well and often I keep the victim isolated from her own community for extended periods of time. The longer I do that, the more money I will receive.

What about the actual women and men I target for my scams? I have both in my radar. The men I target with female fake profiles with nice photos of models found online. Women are targeted with fake profiles of authorative looking male persons with suitable stolen photos. What do I think of them? Some women are rich bitches and some men are fools. Some targets present me with an intellectual challenge. Mostly I look at them as just sheep. I prefer intellectual victims to sheep as it is more entertaining. Either way, both men and women fall with all the predictability my sales marketing skills can give me. I take pride in outsmarting each target. Then I move on to the next one without much thought. My life is a continuous party. Lately, though, I have been considering moving on with the new and more prosperous possibilities scamming offers.

What I am now considering is joining the ranks of Yahoo Boys and even the more advanced organised training programs. The training is very professional and will help me to see my personal actions as a scammer as professional work opportunity. In that program I get trained to perform a variety of different types of online fraud. From simple romance scams to large financial scams. I could join a host of people who develop and create more scams that flow directly from the online actions that we closely monitor. It would be more challenging and the money would be safer. These organisations are very strict and it would mean that I would never get out of the organisation, unless I get arrested with my group. The personal money laundering would be harder then and if the taxation people find out that you have income but have not paid taxes, you can lose your whole fortune.

I am also considering using voodoo. With the help of a spiritual guide, I can raise the stakes and support my psyche. I could be even more confident in my approach. I know that the more trustworthy I sound to the victim, the easier it is to speed up the money flow. However, with this approach I will have to pay a high price to the shamans and it might stress me psychologically to hear the shaman's suggestions and warnings.

However, life is an open book. Particularly on this side of the world. I am living the golden time of my life–I have the money and the fame I deserve. The bad times come if they may. So, no need to worry. Life is short, the risks are worth taking and who cares what happens tomorrow.

CHAPTER 10

Thinking about Recovery through Transformative Thinking

Up until now in this book, we have been focusing on the different realities we face when trying to understand the common denominator for engaging in romance scams, writing romance books, and experiencing pornography. We have come to conclude, through modern research into what is happening in our brains when we are engaged in the pursuit of pleasure, that it is, in fact, the brain itself that is the shared promoter. We have also come to understand how some of the techniques are similar in all these industries. Pursuing any of them fires the same kind of impulses in our brains and thus creates comparable results in our hormonal balance. That then enables those who have the agenda to use their knowledge and skills for their own benefit. Now the question is this: How is it possible for victims to survive and even recover from such an ordeal, be it a scam, a porn addiction, or even overstimulation by reading romantic novels? Would we, if we were aware of all things around us, be able to use this information as a self-help guide to recovery?

There are so many self-help books around that promote easy ways to recover from whatever; it is like an ever-expanding dieting-help catalogue. How are we to recognise what the right way is and how we can create the best-possible happy endings to our experiences? My resolution is to use my knowledge and skills to transmute the energy I gained from the experience into creative writing. This will enlighten me about the circumstances of the phenomena of romance scams and may also help others who have gone through the same kind of experience move towards recovery. I am using my own experience as an example of how to create a worthy happy ending for my story.

Recently I had an email conversation with my dear friend Gloria. She is a retired professor of Comparative Literature and Women's Studies from the University of Southern California and one of my oldest living feminist friends. We were discussing the version of my book that I had sent to her for comment. This version provided a fairy-tale ending to the short story I had written as a result of my scam experience. I had chosen to look at the affair from a distance and to create a happy ending, no matter what. Our discussion considered how I could make this a transformative experience that would truly help women who are faced with the kind of "viral sexism," rape, and violence that we can encounter through the online opportunities of impulse overflow. I decided to take on the challenge of transformative thinking. I remember the following as an experience of shifting reality whereby I changed my own angle of thought.

I remember that Plato, in his classical work *The Republic*, relates to the limited view by which people in a cave might see the world.[1] People are trapped in the cave and only see the world through the shadows that come from the outside. This is how it is for most of us, limited as we are by our own circumstances, beliefs, cultures, languages, and preferences. When we think of recovery, this limited view can apply to both the scammer and the victim. We can both be limited by our view of the world. We are confined to our own status quo of habits in our own little comfort zone. What can we do?

Plato recommends that we turn around and face the light. That way we gain more knowledge through education, awareness-building, and bigger thinking. Through it all we can find the light, and living in the light means that we must pay attention to detail. A treasured theosophical classic by Mabel Collins, *The Light on the Path*, recommends that the traveller "seek out the way" by "retreating within" and "by advancing boldly without." Joy Mills explains it as meditation and taking action.[2] This is the road I must take, and this book is the result of my contemplation on my experience. What would then be a worthy happy ending for me as a survivor of a romance scam? It should reflect my belief system in a way that would help me and others to recovery. It is a process.

I remember some time in 2014 attending an online webinar entitled *Human Potential Movement w*ith Jean Houston. She was talking about gaining your purpose by connecting with your inner self. In her book *A Passion for the Possible* she asked herself the question, "How do we train ourselves to live in an interconnected world?"³ It is the world of information overflow, where everything is constantly changing and we must make quick decisions in order to keep on top of things. Her solution is to connect with our creativity, to draw from our spontaneous inspiration. According to her, women concentrate on the process, and men concentrate on the product.

I also remember a certain ABC Radio *Late Night Live* program.⁴ It was an interview with this amazing man, George Gittoes, who had just won the 2015 Sydney Peace Prize for his work with young people in war zones. He had worked in Pakistan and was then situated in Afghanistan, in the most Taliban-inhabited city, Jalalabad. In the interview, George Gittoes talks about turning pain into art. He says that the best way to recover from post-traumatic stress is to convert it into writing. "It helps you," he assures. George is convinced that it is the lack of education that enables "this kind of brainwashing," meaning the Taliban-influenced brainwashing of young people. He refers to a Taliban leader's son who is attending his school. The boy highlights his own and his father's contradicting beliefs, saying that he does not believe in anything his father believes in.

In George's school, boys and girls get to do art projects side by side. He strongly recommends writing as cure as "it is the best army against post-traumatic stress." I fully agree. Surviving romance scams can be equated to experiencing post-traumatic stress. George is working with and through the community at the grass-roots level, every day contributing to changing the world. He is well aware that it is not going to happen in his lifetime, but he is committed. These memories lead me to discussing romantic fairy tales.

The question I pose to myself in starting my writing process is this: "What level of romance would I like to show in my happy-ending solution?" Is it a fairy tale, or am I aiming for the transformational storyline to aid understanding of the current human consciousness that sets in place the patriarchally layered thought patterns? There is no escape for anyone. We participate, women and men, in keeping the system going. The most extreme form is the war mentality that permeates masculine thinking and interpretation on manliness. I find it interesting that my scammer posed as a military man.

Literally while I was writing the previous paragraph, a friend posted an article[5] on my Facebook page. The article stated that in my birth country of Finland, due to intimidation from Russia, every single person in the army reserve had been sent a letter with instructions on which regiment or unit they should report to "in case of war." The Defence Forces denied links to the current tense situation with Russia, but the experts disagreed. What was I to think about that as a Finn living abroad? Should I like it that my friend had sent me the link? Where was the Do Not Like button? I had been there, for goodness' sake, marching for peace from Helsinki to Moscow, and I had even composed the marching song! So everybody participates. And even if the article was only propaganda and the intimidation was only words and boasts, it was still intimidation, firmly placed in the patriarchal-war-strategy context.

Now I am wondering why it is that one of the most used storylines in scamming, according to the UK study we have previously discussed, is that of military men looking for love. The reason is obvious. A military man gives the impression of power, dominance, and control to the women who are being sourced for scamming purposes. It also reflects the common storyline of romance novels in which men are protectors of helpless women who need someone to guide them through life—sometimes with violence and often with guns. In sadomasochistic porn, and even in the most common pornographic perception, some level of violence is part of the package, be it insinuated or real.

Recently I read a romance novel by Tillie Cole called *Raze*.[6] It is pretty hard-core for a romance book, but it is a good example of a fairy-tale-happy ending to a story that would otherwise shock the reader. It is the story of a pair of soulmates who come from a mafia background and are ripped apart at a young age. The boy is taught to survive for the sole purpose of killing his opponents in the illegal fighting rings he is forced to be part of, while the girl is forced to suffer at the hands of the presumed new heir to the mafia crown. The pair are destined to accidentally meet again. She recognises him, she saves him, he saves her—and in the end, love conquers all. This is what millions of women read, every day. How would my happy ending be any different?

When starting with my writing process I speculated that if my online affair was a swift one, the recovery should not take too much time from my life. I was thinking that it would be destructive to my soul to wallow in misery for an extended time. I thought this would apply to most people who had suffered as a result of online fraud, especially romance scamming, since many do not report it. But they are left thinking about it and questioning their own capacity to deal with the situation in a positive, empowering way.

On that note, I had a really interesting comment from one of my friends while discussing my manuscript with her. She had found her perfect partner through a long search online. I'd always wondered how it was that she had so many boyfriends, one after the other; it had never occurred to me that she was searching online. She commented that it had taken a long time to find the right one. One of the candidates she had identified as a psychopath, and she advised that there was always was a possibility of something terrible happening to her! She felt that she had been lucky. How many women can relate to her statement that out of ten possibilities online, one is a psychopath and only one might be worthy of consideration as a friend? I myself physically met five men besides my online friend. Two were OK to share lunch with, one was entirely disinterested, and the other two were totally focused on getting laid—not a very good prognosis for meeting the right one through online romance sites.

Writing a book wherein I would share my experience with the world seemed a really good way of recovering. However, as I shared my experience with those around me, I found that it was not enough just to explain and contemplate how the experience fitted into the world as I understood it. I also needed a practical and creative solution to help me leave the romance scam behind me and put it into the right context within my world view.

Let me share with you one of my experiences with the Queensland police fraud support group. This experience cemented my determination to lay out my own solution and really knock my online affair on its head. I wanted to do this in a most practical way so that anyone could use it if they wanted to, right away. This is what happened to me.

The QLD Police Fraud group has a support group that meets every second Saturday of the month at the QLD Police Headquarters in the middle of the Brisbane Central Business District. I learned about it from the *Heads First* series, an ABC TV documentary. I contacted the police call centre to enquire whether the group still was active (this was more than two years after the documentary had been shown). I learned that the group was indeed still active, and eventually I received a call and an invitation to attend. I felt very insecure, as I had told the constable that I was writing a book about fraud, and I wasn't sure how he would take it. I found the group very small in comparison to the problem at hand.

Most of the group members had attended for a very long time. Everyone brought cakes for tea. A couple of people shared that they looked on it more as a social gathering. Many had come a long way, from Sunshine Coast or from the Gold Coast. There were about ten people present, including the police officers and the psychologist. I felt out of place.

On that day, most of the discussion was led by a police psychologist. We used the *PRO (Promoting Resilient Officers) Participant Workbook* as our guide to recovery.[7] This program is actually designed for newly recruited officers. However, the psychologist explained that it would work if we mentally removed the officer and replaced it with ourselves. The book has seven chapters. We were discussing chapter three, about helpful self-talk. The aim of the exercise was to take the unhelpful thoughts we had about our relationships to the fraud we had suffered and turn them into helpful thoughts. This would enable us to overcome our ordeals, thus turning negative to positive, pessimism into optimism. Honestly, I woke up crying for two nights in the row afterwards. Why was that?

I could tell that my resentment levels towards what was being advised were just over the top. According to the workbook and the psychologist, it was helpful to accept that "at the end of the day, we are all just mediocre, and that's OK." According to the book and the psychologist, we were not supposed to be "love slops" nor were we to be "comfort slops." We were not to demand that life should be easy for us or that we should not have to endure any discomfort. And most of all, we should not be demanding that the world be fair. In fact, the psychologist said, "Where the hell is it written that the world must be fair? Nowhere!" I was really questioning how these comments would relate to the victims of romance scams.

It seemed that, according to the workbook, we should take our cue from Malcolm Fraser, who said, "Life wasn't meant to be easy," and from M. Scott Peck, who has written, "Life is difficult." We should accept ourselves on the basis that we are human, unique, and alive, and we should acknowledge that life is full of frustrations. At the same time, we should put ourselves "in the driver's seat" by accepting our own thoughts, feelings, and behaviours as they came. It was a sort of twisted Rogarian psychological view.

I can pinpoint the source of my resentment to this attitude on my feminist background. I cannot see that keeping the status quo intact would help in any way to solve the problem of inequality or suffering in this world. I would go for taking action towards change instead of accepting the inevitable.

Now, this might apply when building resilience in police officers, but I would definitely also go for encouraging a more fun, empowering, and creative option for those in my situation. One way would be by creating the best possible romance book or happy-ending scenario for you—the reader—out of your own experience. Another way would be to look at it as it is: a wake-up call to action to create a more humane world, without discrimination and sexism.

My strategy for attempted healing is based on my realisation that instead of holding onto negative thoughts I should create a positive memory for myself. This approach also appeared to resonate with others, for when I attended at the fraud support group a second time and presented my idea, it was taken very well, and I was really encouraged to continue.

In fact, my inspiration to write a romance story inspired by my experience came directly from my elder son's comment that I should not go and read all the reports about the scammer on the www.scammers. com site. Instead, he wanted me to remember all the romancing the scammer had done and keep my good feelings about it. This also led to us discussing how I might illustrate the chapter on scammers in an artistic way, to tell the story and further progress ideas and information on the subject. With both of my sons I had invigorating discussions about what kind of documentaries or movies we could create from my experience with the scammer.

When I have told people about my son's suggestion, many have reacted to it by saying that I have a very supportive and loving family. That is true. My family also wants to shield me from suffering.

We also need to uncover the bias that surrounds us in the world and work our way out of our misery by empowering our souls to further action and compassion. This will make the world a better place despite the great sorrow it may bring. It could be an empowering experience in itself.

My son's suggestion coincided with my reading of Napoleon Hill's classic book *Think and Grow Rich*. I quickly realised that—despite half of the book discussing the possibility of transmuting the emotions of sex and love into creative abundance—most people, while acknowledging the role of Hill's amazing insights to enhance their own lives, have totally omitted this aspect of the book.

It could be, of course, that most of us do not have muses to inspire us to achieve what we want in life. Love, combined with sexual arousal, is a powerful emotion. According to modern brain research, it can fill our brains with such a high that it is compared to a heroin high—it takes a lot to come down from. In the case of this book, talking about this is appropriate. In fact, I feel that it is just the thing to do.

Let's concentrate on thinking about this in another way. In doing so, we might come to the conclusion that if the online dating affair has really served its purpose to the scammer, the target of the scam will be so filled with hormones that his or her "reason" will have been dismissed. He or she will be working from basic instincts—the "lizard brain"—and not from the frontal cortex, which would make a rational conclusion and recognise the scam as a scam with more than enough evidence provided to support the claim.

In some ways we could say that the scammer has taken the position of the muse. In fact, I actually told my scammer that he was my muse and that he was flooding me with hormones that could be transmuted to creativity, just like those famous stories of the muses of artists and authors we read about and admire so much. Here's what I wrote to him at the time:

You know that I am totally in awe of you, Stephen, my love. I do not care who you really are and what you are doing, it is You and the emotions you evoke in me that I am fascinated with. I am grateful as you have already helped me, so much, by awakening the emotion and the inspiration I need to get on with my life.

I cannot help you with money but I can help you with emotionalising for you what you want, and you can do the same for me. Because you do it to me, with your voice. I have said it many times. And OMG you do it to me with the texts. You can really inspire my brain to great heights with that. And since meeting you online, I have not read any romance books, not one. That is a great achievement. You have really done a great job at participation with the texts and how they really push the hormones up to my brain.

It is entirely possible to create our own stories by using the experience, by remembering the emotions that the affair raised in us, and by applying the same methods famous people have used to create anything they wanted—from lucrative business models to fine art, music, and stories.

There are many famous writers who are thought to have had someone or something as inspiration for at least some of their artistic process, starting from Shakespeare and Jane Austen and maybe ending with the thought of the ancient creative genius that Elizabeth Gilbert called back into the creative process in her famous TED talk in 2009, called "Your Elusive Creative Genius."[8]

In hindsight, I could say that by the time we got to discussing aspects of the scamming process and creativity, I already had recognised the scam. I had moved from thinking about my scammer as a person to appreciating the inspiration he provided for me to move away from my state of emotional despair to a more positive frame of mind.

There is also the alternative suggestion that the happy ending for the woman in my story might be to understand the world around her, so she can create her own contentment—without the added bias of the patriarchal world that prescribes a romantic ending as a solution to every misery of the world.

What I found is that the method the scammer used—that is, getting his/her target to a position of automatic sympathy for his/her imaginary plight and automatically parting from their money to help a lover in need—could also be a cue for cure for the victims of fraud. For myself, I developed a nine-step process to think about before I wrote my first story.

1: Accept where you are right now. Map your current feelings and write them down.

2: Think of what was so good about the thoughts and feelings that you had when the affair was at its best. How did you feel? How did you react to his/her messages, and how did you answer his/ her persuasion? What did you do that was so good that you took action without thought? The goal is to get aligned with those feelings and record them for yourself.

3: Let go of the negative by changing your story. Ask yourself, "How do I let go of the negative feelings?" The answer will be, by changing your own thoughts. Keep a journal if you want or need to.

4: Map the positive moments from your experience onto a timeline. You could use storytelling software or just notepaper. The goal is to gather the sequence into a timeline.

5: Go back to your memories of the good times, and map your own imagination of the happy ending into a timeline that will logically follow the real story from the scammer.
6: Combine the storylines from the point where you realised that it was a scam. Disregard the disappointment, and concentrate on the whole positive experience. It does not need to be elaborate. It is your story. It is your best romantic outcome. Write it out as an outline.
7: Plan the outline. What will you take from the actual affair? Are there letters, conversations, calls, or whatever, that you can use as easy material?
8: Put your story together. Join our creative online peer-group workshop to discuss the storyline, get feedback, and support each other.
9: Write your story

CHAPTER 11

Love Online: The Fairy Tale

There is this man and this woman I know.

The woman is an academic and really smart but has fallen into depression after her mother's death and after being diagnosed with fibromyalgia. The man is a street-smart survivor of the circumstances of his birth. Later he joined the army and served in several war zones. He became hardened and worn by violence. Both the man and the woman were lonely.

They met on the Internet, through one of those romance sites, romance.com or some such. Otherwise, I doubt that they ever would have met. Here's to the efficiency of the digital media!

The guy swept the woman off her feet by the power of the clichés in the written word. Just like that! Amazing to hear! Usually she was so smart and always a little apprehensive of the world around her. That surely came from researching such subjects as violence and pornography. For years she had done that. She was always ready to start preaching about the dangers of the world. Her downfall was her enthusiasm for the belief that goodness will rule after all.

Anyway, all I want to say is that it could happen. And it did.

The man wrote her really, really cliché-filled emails. They could have been cut and pasted from anywhere; probably he has learned all that from studying marketing. He went on and on about respect, family values, and how he wanted to find his soulmate. He marvelled at how the "circumstances of the online matching system" had brought them together so easily. He also said that he was ready to fall in love and take care of her. Just like that, provided that he could retire from the army as soon as possible.

At first the woman felt sorry for the man. He had had such a hard and lonely life and was always in danger. He had lost his wife and daughter to a car accident, just as he had lost his parents earlier in life. His uncle, who ended up raising him to maturity, was quite a character, full of strict orders and no love. Poor man!

Well, anyway. They started mailing each other most intensively, several emails a day. In no time at all, they both felt as if they had known each other a very long time, maybe months—even years if you counted it in snail mail. So, with the real-time digital media's help, they fell in love in two weeks flat. Fair dinkum! I am telling you the truth.

The woman felt that the man was just right for her. Very quickly she was certain that he could be trusted with her most intimate secrets. The man seemed to be on board. He wrote her wonderfully romantic emails, texted her amorous words she adored, had a voice to die for on the phone, and carried on Skype conversations with her that were pure lustful fun. Oh. My. God! What do you think a girl could do in a situation like that but surrender? And surrender she did.

It was as if she were obsessed. Obviously the lizard brain had taken over; there was no room for the frontal cortex to give any advice or rational thought. And then the man went to his last mission in Afghanistan. The woman was so stressed and worried that she basically was glued to her phone, waiting for texts, as the man was not within the phone zone.

After three days she got a text saying only that the man has missed her so much and loved her even more. Well, what a relief! At least that was something. It gave her a flicker of hope that all would be well. Psychological manipulation, I'd say, but who's asking?

Anyway! After yet another day, a second message came. The man texted that they were coming back to base, ending the agony for the woman, and making her so happy and even more attached to the guy. After coming back, the man was very weary and not able to tell her much, of course, but was very loving and convincing. He told her that he would leave as soon as the replacement officer arrived. He said that he had already submitted his retirement papers. Getting the replacement person there would take two weeks. The woman was so excited.

She imagined and told me that he would be coming to see her as soon as possible after getting all his affairs organised in the United Kingdom. She was filled with happiness. He had told her that he would always protect her and never let her down and that he would now make it his sole mission to be her loving husband.

She believed him! She fully trusted that it would happen. Can you believe that? This man would first go to the UK, get his affairs in order, fully retire, and then fly off down under to see her and literally sweep her off her feet with the first passionate kiss at the airport. That was his plan. What a fool the woman was, if you want my opinion—but of course you don't. I am only the narrator here.

Anyway, during one crucial Skype conversation, the man opened up to the woman about his worries concerning the political situation in Afghanistan at the time. He was worried that something might turn up that would prevent him from leaving the country and returning to the UK. And then he revealed to her that he was actually more worried about another situation altogether, which was happening in Dubai at that very moment. According to his story, he had sent his medals and other valuables to the UK prior to going on his last mission, and now the UN agent that he had trusted his belongings to was in trouble at the airport, because the customs officials were demanding some extra papers that he had not been prepared for. The agent wanted some money from him to clear the situation, but he was unable to get it there.

Apparently the man had tried everything he could and was very anxious to leave his post, but the replacement person had not yet appeared. In fact, his replacement had been delayed in Iraq. The man was frantic. It turned out that he had some very valuable and secret stuff in his baggage and did not want the customs in Dubai to inspect it, but they would if the money did not arrive. Of course, as a result of the leading conversation, the woman asked what the best solution to the problem would be, fool that she was. The man then had an opportunity to ask for the woman's help. He promised to pay her back immediately, three times over, when he was in London and able to move money around. And the woman believed him—can you believe that? That's when she learned how to transfer money between countries through the Western Union offices.

There were lots of problems associated with sending the money. She should have read the signs, say I. Finally, after a couple of tries and a lot of paperwork, texting, and Skyping, the transfer went through, but did it clear the situation? Not in the least. Now they were asking the High Court to clear the papers, and more money was needed, or at least it was needed for the customs officer who was left there in charge of the baggage, defending it against the threat that it would be examined. If whatever was in there were found to be illegal, the man would be in huge, huge trouble. The woman had no more money, so the baggage stayed there. And then the man disappeared from her radar.

Meanwhile, the woman had left for a conference, so she did not know what was happening. She heard nothing from the man for a few days, and then she got a call from Ghana—Accra, to be precise. Apparently, the man had left Afghanistan and flown to Ghana, of all places, to get his stuff organised. What do you think of that? Suspicious, say I—but again, I am not being asked in any way.

Anyway, the story continues, and the plot thickens.

The man then tells the woman that he is still coming to her, as soon as he is able after the situation with the baggage is satisfactorily concluded. He assures her that he is not leaving his baggage to Ghana. But, again, he needs money. According to him, he has used his last five thousand US dollars to diffuse the situation, but this is not enough for the papers, the illegal ones that are needed. Will the woman help? She has no money, so she can't. The man tells her that it is OK, because he doesn't want to lose her over this small matter, as he loves her so much. He says that he will sell all his valuables, including his gold Rolex, to get money. He is so pitiful, and to top it all, he falls ill. It is chicken box, not Ebola.

The woman is devastated. She is just about to give up on their future and says so to the man. He sends her yet another romantic text—would you believe that?—and then goes fishing, of all possible things to do! She doesn't hear from him for weeks. I would say that this would be the right time to give it up, but the woman's heart is persistent.

It is three weeks before he calls her from the UK. London is where he has finally ended up. It turns out that he has found his courage from somewhere and has gotten himself to Britain to face the wrath of the army, who were by this time looking for him. Luckily, he was already technically retired before fleeing from Afghanistan, so they did not reprimand him too badly, although he has a dishonourable discharge.

But what does that matter to him? He is ready for a new life, he says. He can afford it, he says.

Anyway, to cut a long story short, in her imagination it takes him six months to actually arrive at her city down under. She is not fooled any more, and she is not sure how she will take it. She really doesn't know now whether she wants the relationship to continue or not. However, he convinces her to meet him at the airport. Finally, she gets that kiss. Afterwards, she takes him home, and they sit on her balcony drinking red and white wine and discussing things, and he convincingly explains to her what actually did occur. She gets her money back. And in the end, she decides to follow through to a happy ending, if possible. So they go for a road trip to Alice Springs to meet his grandfather.

It takes six weeks. She gets used to him. The sex is good. They continue to travel around Australia to see his pals and other things. It takes a few months and gives them time to get to know each other for real.

After nine months, he proposes. Can you believe that? She accepts. They arrange a wedding. She gets a designer ring that incorporates a lapis lazuli stone. It is the very same one that he carried home from Afghanistan in his precious baggage.

She tells me she is happy. It's a romantic ending, hey?

CHAPTER 12

Discussion on the Possibility of Alternative Storylines through Social Change

All my life I have been one who resisted the norm by choosing to represent those who were oppressed for some political view or just for being of the wrong gender. At fourteen, I started a youth movement for freedom of thought, after someone in my school said to me that I did not need to think for myself; I just needed to follow his party's lead, and everything would be OK. At nineteen, while studying English philology at university, I complained to the dean that there were only men's books on the program and asked where the women were. The university's faculty responded by letting me come up with an alternative program, and my professor pointed me to the newly formed women's studies group. At twenty-five I wrote the song "Women and Children Do not Have to Think." It was about the effect that WWII had had on women and children of my family. That song was published in several peace publications, including the Finnish book entitled *Women's Peace Songs*.[1] Why have I now forgotten that and written a full fairy-tale type of romance for myself?

For starters, let's consider the characters in my story. If I reflect on it, I could say that the storyline would be more meaningful if I imagined an alternative that incorporated a social-change agenda.

The character of the military man does not come across as real, and I also note that I totally overstepped the scammer and the possibility of him recovering from his scamming addiction. Would that even be possible?

Let's look at what is happening today around the world. Let's focus for a while on how patriarchal, warlike thought patterns are affecting our everyday lives, if not directly, then through the world news and social media. Let's prove the point that Gerda Lerner made in her book, *The Creation of Patriarchy*, which was already discussed in an earlier chapter. Gerda states that, in a patriarchy, men's autonomy is embodied by the concept of honour. Those men who cannot protect their women— wives, children, and others— lose their honour. Women do not have that autonomy. Women's honour, on the other hand, lies in their virginity and/or availability for sexual services. In patriarchal societies, men are predisposed to terrorise women by physical or psychological rape. The assumption is that, once impregnated, the enslaved women will shift their alliance to their new masters. Lerner is a historian who writes about the roots of slavery, and she talks about 2500 BC and the first century AD, but let's see if anything has changed today[2]

Just recently, in the month of May, 2015, I read about women being rescued from Boko Haram captivity in Nigeria.[3] Over the years, rebels have abducted thousands of women and girls, routinely raped them, forced them into sexual slavery, and married them off to their own militias. When rescued, most are found to be pregnant or to already have a child. I read that the rebels assume that because the women and their own society will not accept the children, these children will reject their mothers and will eventually be easy targets to be recruited for war. The same tactics are used by the ISIS organisation and others in the Middle East. The same tactics are used by the pornography industry, especially by the human trafficking industry, and by scammers everywhere. The same tactics are used with domestic violence, which is reported to be much larger-scale than before anticipated, in ordinary homes throughout the world. The same tactics are used by the Catholic Church-driven laws in South America and around the world, where women can be jailed for forty years for miscarrying after being raped.⁴ Some of the romance books I have read have actually taken their inspiration from real research into human trafficking, and even though the subject matter is converted to a grizzly romance novel, it shows off those who are writing the books in such a way as to try to humanise the issue and bring it to the reader's attention.

In 2004, I spent three months in India, at the School of the Wisdom at the Theosophical Society headquarters in Chennai. Our teacher was Dr Satish Inamdar, who is the director of the Krishnamurti School in Bangalore. We had a long discussion about violence in the slums of India. He commented that the violence against women in the slums of the large cities there is not 99 per cent, it is 100 per cent. He was quite adamant about that. He found it very disturbing. Since then I have read about much good being done in slums. This includes helping the children of prostitutes to break the cycle of poverty through education and other opportunities, the movement towards setting up businesses through micro loans, and much more.

In the *Voice Male: The Untold Story of the Pro-Feminist Men's Movement*,⁵ I read about challenging rape culture and violence against women. They say that because 97 per cent of the violence is committed by men, it is a men's issue. There is a whole movement to consider. The International Center for Research on Women (ICRW) has called on men to form MenEngage groups around the world to educate boys and men in overcoming violence. The groups are everywhere, though not in Ghana, where my scammer is from. I find that there are many men who fight for freedom from their patriarchal thought patterns. One of them is Dr Denis Mugwege, of whom I also read in one of the articles in *Voice Male* magazine.⁶ For years in his career as a gynaecologist and obstetrician, he has been engaged in "sewing up women's vaginas" in the Congo "as fast as the militias are ripping them apart," according to the article. He is a hero in the field of men against men's violence against women.

So there is a slight possibility for my scammer to engage in social change, although it is a diminutive one. The alternative storyline will also have to bypass him. But what about the woman? How will I write a happy ending for her? Could this be imagined better through an alternative ending?

To start with my process, I wrote three versions of the romance novel meant to be part of this book. There is a really long version, which basically preserves all the conversations and notes that I have of the online affair. It is around thirty thousand words, which is about the size of the type of romance novel I usually read and enjoy. In hindsight, it is the historian in me that wants to record everything as it is and who has a hard time concluding or finishing the thing because life just interferes.

The second version is the edited version—a ten-thousand-word novella that I sent to a few friends to comment on.

The shorter version still faithfully follows what really happened. My explanation of what had occurred previously and what I imagined would happen afterwards is included in the prologue and epilogue. I edited down the profusion of clichés that our conversations consisted of; he had been cutting and pasting words that I now recognised from other letters to other victims of fraud, while I had been trying to figure what was in it at all. That version could be of interest to a researcher or someone who has experienced a similar scam and wants to compare notes. I have since distanced myself so far from the affair that it seems like a dream, yet the historian in me persisted.

My emotions were many, ranging from wondering how on earth I had fallen for it, through to recognising that at the time it had been a gut reaction to enjoy the journey and fully emerge in the "now" of it. I appreciate that it was exhilarating for my hormones as well.

A conversation with a friend got me thinking that there should be something more. I decided to try a short story instead. The result was presented in the previous chapter. In that fairy-tale version, I participated with the status quo of the romance script and ended up making the scammer's profiled military man into an unworthy hero. How could I make it better and more reflective of my own conviction that recovery is impossible when we do no more than scratch the surface, play the game, and bypass the obvious? I tried to do so by thinking about the previously presented nine steps, as played out through two scenarios. Would there be a difference in my thinking of the happy endings, and could I work towards a transformative solution? Here is the summary of what I did with my writing process:

In my first attempt, I basically accepted the current norms of our society and tried to preserve the status quo, writing a love story that would have a happy ending in a romantic, conventional way. My second story was all about transforming the characters, through lateral thinking, to a better and more emotionally satisfying new beginning. The best and most positive experience for me in both storylines was my emotional wake-up call to the world we live in. I moved from acceptance to creative action that was really satisfying to my soul.

At first the only negative thoughts that I had about my online affair were around the fact that as a young person I had been part of the women's peace movement, and having an affair with a military person, even if it was online, was a huge thing to get past. I managed to turn my thoughts around that, too, mostly because in the beginning I felt sorry for the man.

For the plotline, I had two choices. I could choose a military man, such as the one the scammer had created for me, and have him realise his folly and come to the woman a changed man. Alternatively, I could choose that the woman would find fulfilment and the courage within to take action in some worthy cause, and through that she would meet another man. He would be one who has already had his struggle and transformed into a pro-feminist, working with men against violence against women. For inspiration I read the love story of the famous feminist Merlin Stone and her partner of thirty-two years, Lenny Schneir, from a book called *Merlin Stone Remembered*.[7] The story is told from Lenny's point of view. It is his love letter to a great woman. The storyline describes a man changing, through love and understanding, from a misogynist to not only a pro-feminist but a Goddess-loving man as well. It is a true description of the transformative power of love.

Merlin Stone's importance was in the Goddess Movement and her findings about the Goddess. My greatest memory from her ideas was the reintroduction of the concept of historical time that should not be viewed only as Before Christ (BC) and Anno Domino (AD), after Christ, but from the time of building the first city states—some eight thousand years before.

The story restored my belief in the possibility of romance. I also meditated on the concept of courage; what is it that gets us to do what we do each day and how we can be courageous enough to stick to our principles.

While rewriting the storyline, I was able to revisit the positive emotions that had helped me overcome the trauma rather than wallowing in despair.

The real happy ending will be tested by time. Have I been able to leave the online affair behind me? How much have I been able to contribute to helping others do the same? What has been my action?

In the end, I chose to write the woman as the hero, a survivor of her circumstances, and the instigator for change. She is able to turn her life around and only then meets a more suitable man. He also has had his struggles to be himself in the patriarchal world, and with him she can develop a loving partnership. I took my own advice by joining peer groups.

A dear friend with a life-coaching business invited me to be part of her first group program. It helped me to reconnect with my inner purpose in life and revaluate what I wanted my future to look like. My coach inspired me to keep on writing, and the encouragement of my peer group also was such that I was stimulated to continue. I recognise that, English being my second language, the writing process has been much more challenging than I had first imagined it would be. My coach helped me overcome the fear of expressing my thoughts in my second language.

The group that has been reading the chapters and giving me feedback has also been vital in the writing process. Without their kind words and encouragement, I might have given up altogether after my curiosity about the world around us had been satisfied. Now, thanks to my reconsidering and rewriting, the story has matured and developed into something I am really proud of.

The Queensland Police fraud prevention support group has given me the background and encouragement to see that something is done— and to see that *more* can be done to help people cope with their ordeals and even manage them and heal from them. I have realised that for some people it can take a long time, but it has led many to a new career and a new outlook on life.

CHAPTER 13

Love Online: The Alternative Short Story

I know this woman. Actually, you know her too.

She is a wreck! The woman, I mean. Really, truly traumatised. Kept crying while relating her story to me. At first she thought that telling white lies would be the best thing. She wanted to save herself from the embarrassment. It did not work, did it? She regretted this, and then she came out with it.

I respect her. I had had my suspicions—but as only a narrator. What could I do? Nothing. Nobody asks my opinion, do they now? The stories are theirs to tell. They belong to the people who share them with me. This woman wanted me to know her real pain, her disappointment and sorrow for the world we live in—that it could be like this.

Turns out that she had met this one man online, on some romance site, romance.com or some such. She had fallen for him hook, line, and sinker. He was a fisherman. No, not really, but it did turn out that what he was doing online is called "phishing." He had been looking for vulnerable people to take advantage of. Like many others, he posed as a military man, in the British peacekeeping troops in Afghanistan.

First the woman was quite wary, because she was an academic and quite smart, but obviously she had not been smart enough to see the signs. Well, anyway, the man had posed as half Australian, half

British. He had told her he was born near her own town, so she'd felt they had a connection through similar upbringing. And she had felt sorry for him for being so alone in the world. Just like her—beyond lonely.

Well, anyway. They started emailing each other. The messages kept flying through the cyberspace most intensively. In two weeks they had exchanged as many messages as could be compared to several months of letter-writing through the snail mail. He wrote to her in clichés that could have been cut and pasted from many sources, but they were constructed in a way that she really fell for. He was a master of his trade. She wrote to him earnestly, thinking that he was the real thing, someone to give her trust to. How wrong could she be!

He swept her off her feet in no time at all with sweet words and a telephone voice to die for. OMG! She kept reading and rereading his messages and getting high on the hormones that their conversations and messages produced in her brain. Well, she had fun, and she was happy! I give her that.

Her family was very supportive and pleased that she had found someone who would be a nice companion for her. She had been alone so long, just caring for everybody and not thinking about romance other than through romance book-reading. Well, I would say that somewhere along the way she had convinced herself that there was a romantic, happy ending possible for everyone and that you should just take the opportunity when it presented itself. Plus, she was severely in pain, did I mention that? So, I am giving her a little slack, although if asked, I would have warned her immediately. But I was not asked, was I now?

Anyway, the story continues. The man had promised to come to her and literally sweep her off her feet at the airport with a lover's kiss. And she was waiting for him to do just that. In fact, she believed in him and trusted that after his retirement from the army he would go back to UK, as promised, and get his affairs in order, as promised, and then travel to down under. They would meet, drink some wine on her patio, and there would be a happy ending to it all. She was looking forward to everything she imagined it could be. However, some grey clouds had appeared by the time the man went to his last mission in Afghanistan. She was most anxious for him. After a few days he sent her a text message, saying only that they were coming to their home base and that he loved her so much. She was the best he could have and the only one he was thinking of while away searching for Taliban hideouts. Well, at least she had some relief. He sounded so sweet!

He came back to base and only then related to her his worries about the situation in Afghanistan. He was worried that something would keep him there, due to the political situation. He knew that being worried for him would make her more attached to him—and it worked. Actually, he was fishing for her sympathy for other purposes. Namely, he had another problem altogether.

He told her how before going to his mission he had trusted his treasured belongings to a UN agent, who was supposed to take them to the UK for him. He further told her that he had gotten a reward from the Afghan government for helping in some peace negotiations, as he could speak a few languages, including the local dialect. He was afraid that the reward would be lost while he was on his mission.

Well, well, the plot thickens.

She asked what the problem was, of course, and he told her that the agent had been delayed at the Dubai Airport because of some papers that he had been unprepared for. He asked for her help in getting some money to the agent to defuse the situation. He would be unable to get money himself because of his situation. And can you believe it? She trusted him and helped him by sending the money. She thought that he would come and pay her back immediately. What a fool she was.

Luckily, a doubt started in her brain, and she began to research the man, despite his previous warning not to do just that.

Anyway, you would think that that was that and happy ending, right there—but no, not at all. Immediately more money was needed. She did not have any, so she could not help, and she was going away to a conference, so she missed his messages. Lucky for her. A few days went by without him contacting her, and then she got a call from Ghana. It turns out the man had left Afghanistan in haste and ended up in Accra. She could not quite believe it and finally felt that something was off. So she asked her son for help. And while she was waiting for results, the man got into more trouble in Accra and asked for even more money. She did not have it and said so. He said that it was OK and that he loved her anyway. He would sell his valuables, but after that, he would need more money. She was frustrated. Her son searched the net and in no time at all found that the man was a scammer. He told her to block the man and advised her to only remember the best parts of him romancing her.

Poor woman, she was devastated, but she was brave. Immediately she blocked the scammer from her contacts and stopped thinking about him and the affair. She was not interested, she said, in finding him, the real man. She had had enough, she told me. She would just leave it be. But that well-used tactic did not work for her, did it now? Something kept bothering her, every day. She had a doubt, and sorrow grew in her heart. She asked herself how it had happened, and why, and what kind of world we lived in where women were so vulnerable. They apparently are so predictable that they become easy prey for people who want to take advantage of them. And anyway, where had her own dreams gone? When she left me, she was still crying and so very down that I was worried for her. Occasionally I would think about her and wonder where she was, what she was doing, and whether she really was getting over her trauma. Two years passed. One day she called me, sounding very much herself again. How wonderful for her! Would I join her for a cuppa? Of course I would.

We met at our usual place. She had moved but had come to town on business, and she looked gorgeous—absolutely fabulous and smiling from her ear to ear, like her usual self. I was so pleased. She showed me her engagement ring with a blue designer stone. She smiled and smiled! She treated me to champagne. I asked what had happened.

She told me that at first, after our previous meeting so long ago, she had been very, very depressed. She had felt that her world had ended, not only because the man she had met online had turned out to be a scammer but because the world as she knew it had changed, and she had not paid attention. She had not been able to recognise it for what it was. She had used to be a fighter, but something had come over her and dampened her spirit and her ability to take action. She thought that she had always been courageous in her actions. But now she felt defeated by the world around her. She just felt the sorrow of the world, and it was a heavy burden to bear.

She said that she had tried everything but nothing had worked. She'd thought that she would perish. Then her grandchildren had arrived from abroad. Looking at the new generation, she'd found that she could not just sit and take it as it came; she had to get a new direction. She decided to find her courage by taking a stand on her own behalf. Her first action was to move.

She chose a smaller community, nearer to the grandchildren so that she could see them and play with them and feel the joy of living in the *now* with them. It helped. She was happier. Her second action was to become better aligned with her original purpose, the one she had forgotten. Immediately she met some great women and joined their group. Her confidence grew. Once again she felt empowered.

Her third action was to start writing. Researching was what she could do well. So she did just that. She found that the world had changed, and the outlook had changed, and not one person, apart from some rare futurists, could tell anything about the direction the world was inclined to head in. She also found that what she now knew about the world was much more accurate than that which she had learned when she was young. This was because instead of being hidden it was now all revealed, mostly in cyberspace. She found the world had changed into being more transparent and accountable—as well as more predatory. That gave her even more courage to get her thoughts out there. To take action. Once again she was convinced that there must be something an individual could do with other individuals. The women's group was a blessing in her life.

Then, unexpectedly, it seemed she was ready, for she met this very interesting fellow. It was at some unnamed conference where she gave a speech. To her amazement, he identified himself as a pro-feminist right away. He was working with men to encourage them to re-evaluate their lives and see beyond their limits. After a day, they joined with a group of other interested people for coffee and ended up the last ones there, discussing their interests until midnight. The next day they met for lunch and continued over dinner. It was strange. She felt strange. He felt he liked her—really! She liked him too. OMG! This time it might work. She was truly nervous. He invited her to the movies. It was like a date. What could she say? What could she do? She said yes!

I cannot imagine why it is with women that they feel so nervous and immediately so unsure of themselves when a good-looking man shows interest, real interest. It was as if she were not aware how beautiful she was or how her inner power was shining through. Luckily for her, she took the chance. She admitted to me that it soon become personal. Suddenly, their relationship transformed into being more about attraction and mutual respect than pretending to show a professional facade.

They had what you would call a few dates, and then they went away for a weekend together. And that was that. They were a couple, inseparable after that. They both had their own interests and work, but now they could combine and start planning what they could do together. Two heads instead of the one, two bodies instead of one. They decided to get engaged and maybe marry, sometime in the future. She got the ring with the designer blue lapis lazuli stone to celebrate that recovery is possible for us all if we apply our spirits, our souls, and our sinews.

I became quite interested in finding out more about the man she said she was engaged to. I was sceptical and wanted to meet him. She called my bluff by saying that that was fair enough, and she called him. A man sitting at the outer terrace answered. I could see him from where we were sitting. He looked like a man of Scandinavian origins. He joined us. She said she'd known that I would ask about it and was happy to introduce us.

At first he was very courteous and formal, but with some coaxing he shared his story. I was very interested to know why he identified himself as a pro-feminist and what had led him to my friend.

He told me that his father had been a famous linguist in Sweden, a phonetics professor, and his mother had been an English teacher at a local high school. It had used to bother him that his father always referred to his mother as just a teacher. That contributed to his realisation at an early age that spouses had different status in a marriage. According to him, included in his lectures his father had had a standard derogatory comment about women's independence. The father would say that when a woman became liberated, the tone of her voice would lower. The son had detested his father's patronising his mother. That, he said, he would always remember, and immediately he had decided to do better.

His father had been the celebrity of the family, but his mother had gone to women's groups and taken him with her. She had loved Virginia Woolf, Sylvia Plath, Simone de Beauvoir, and the early Swedish female writers like Elin Wägner. He had liked her mother's friends better than his father's pompous ones. When he was a boy, that is.

Apparently, by the time he was a teenager, the family had moved to Britain due to the father's work, and he ended up at a university there. Eventually, he got into such an argument with his father that he was thrown out of their home. For a short period of time he had experienced what homelessness in London was like—because he had been embarrassed to tell his friends why he had left home. Soon enough, though, he had gotten a place to stay. However, he had spent enough time on the streets to realise how many young people there were who were in trouble. He had started volunteering with a group that worked with homeless youth, especially boys. There had been a lot of violence among them, and drug abuse and trafficking. He had not talked to his father for years.

Meanwhile, having taken enough abuse, his mother had finally left his father and set up a household with a friend who also had divorced recently. That is how this man had met his first wife. She was a daughter of his mother's friend. Somehow, they had fallen into the sort of routine that was expected from them, working to advance their careers and make something out of themselves. It had not lasted for long. Luckily, there were no children, although he said he later had a daughter from a short-term fling. She was the light of his life, he said.

He had tried to be a man of modern times. But it was hard work to take on the expectations, and finally he had chosen his work on the streets as his main focus. He had realised that violence was a major problem—the way we talk to each other, the way we express anger and fear. It was mostly men who would turn to violence, so he had started working with young men and anger-management issues. He then moved on to adult men who wanted to break the cycle of domestic violence. Somewhere along the line, he had started identifying himself as pro-feminist, first because he felt that it was all he could do to support women and later because he felt it to be the right kind of definition for who he was and is. It was a commitment, he said. He was lucky, though: he was tall, fair, and rather easy on the eye. Trustworthy.

At the conference where he had met my friend, he had been blown away by her brains and her beauty, he said, and he smiled at her, tenderly. She literally snort at him. "He thought I was sexy," she said.

"You are very sexy," he confirmed. We all laughed. They looked to be in love, confident, and with purpose. When they left, I knew she was happy in her new beginning.

CHAPTER 14

Concluding the Journey and Moving on with Life

> One day a woman asked her lover, "Do you love me more than you love yourself?" He replied, "I love you so much that I am full of you from head to toe. There is no distinction between loving you and loving myself; loving myself is loving you."
>
> —Rumi[1]

As I arrive at the end of my book, I must confess that conclusions are always hard for me. The challenge lies in deciding that it is the end and that now I need to say something wise to put a full stop to it (instead of continuing to find yet another angle to my storyline). My aim with this book was to share with you my experience of romance scams and the world we live in. My desire was to achieve some kind of recovery that would allow me to let go of thinking about the romance scam I was the target of.

The title of the book indicates that I now know something about recovering from romance scams, something about how to keep my dignity and to break out of the victim mode. If I have been successful in sharing my experience with the audience, readers will also feel that they have received something to spark their inspiration and prompt them to action for themselves. I truly hope that is the case.

Writing this book has been a twelve-month journey for me, much like bringing forth a child would be. Sometimes it has been painful, but mostly it has been joyful because of all the new contacts and all the new insights that I have arrived at along the way. I am convinced this will continue to be a great journey as the book is printed and published, and I will be able to engage in many conversations about the book and the message it brings to the world. I hope the reader will realise that it is my earnest opinion, and only mine, and that everyone can have their own and still be able to recover. There are countless ways to look at the issue. I have shared my angle and my solution. I will be delighted to exchange views in the future with interested readers and others as well.

Still, after all my experience with romance scams, I remain romantic at heart. I firmly believe in the good of the heart and that compassion and kindness will bring us forward more than conflict and destruction will. But I am very practical and have chosen my ranks. I will stand on the barricades with those who I believe have chosen the right action— that is, to do something about the injustice of the world we live in. My way is to share my experience and make the reader aware. I am all for education and for developing skills that will help to bring forward the happy ending I so long for.

The final question before me is this: Did I truly recover, and what actually was it that I needed to recover from? The only thing I can be absolutely sure about is that I am partial to happy endings. I like romance books because the hero or heroine gets the love of their life. And I can make sure that I am entertained in that process.

I am not entertained by tragedies. They make me want to act on behalf of the victims. It is a gut reaction, and I cannot help it. These are sad situations. But the positive in that is that it can make me think. It is an opportunity to find new solutions towards happier endings—one at a time.

I would say that after writing this book I am fully recovered from my online affair. However, it will still leave me wondering what more I could contribute to the world with regard to changing the underlying social infrastructure. I am convinced that I can only do what is right in my life by educating others through this book, whatever future it brings me.

And lastly, I can only thank you for reading this. It was a pleasure to connect with you.

CHAPTER 15

Tips for the Future Avoidance of Becoming a Victim of Fraud

The Internet scams are many and varied. They are spreading like fire, all over the Internet, all over the world as fast as the use of the Internet gets easier and more accessible. The Internet fraudster are very equal in they approach. No-one, nowhere in the world is excluded from their range. This might be the most inclusive approach ever. Nobody anywhere online is left behind from their careful scrutiny. Everybody knows somebody who has been scammed. There are so many ways to end up as scammers pray.

According to the RomanceScamsNow.com, one Internet scam happens every five seconds around the world every day. There are over 15, 5 million attempts for scamming per day, over 2740 people end up as new scam victims, less than three fraudsters will be arrested but four fraud victims will commit suicide. Thus it is important to mind about online scamming and fraud. Everyone using Internet needs to prepare for them. Every person needs to learn the necessary skills to avoid scams and escape from becoming the next victim of Internet fraud. Every Internet or Smart Phone user needs to pay special attention to learning to use their devices in a correct way to preserve their own safety.

We must remember that scammers and fraudsters fund a lot of worldwide terrorism as well as the drug and human trafficking trade.

Main Categories for Internet Fraud:

Email Scams:
These scams are known to all. They include the Nigerian and the You-got-inheritance scams. In them someone will email you to tell you that you can acquire millions of dollars, you only have to follow their advice and/or steps to do so. These kind of scams rely on the nativity and the creed of the human mind.

Computer Scams:
The Computer Scams or the cold calls, where people are spontaneously offered help or sold services or stuff are the second type of scams. They are happening all over the world and are most always caused by humans. They include blackmail or pressure by the scammers with malware, viruses or the loss of computer files.

Romance Scams:
'I love you. Send me money'! Here is the romance scam basically in the nutshell. They start in many ways through the social media, different dating sites or through emails. The scammers pose as fake persons. They trust that the victims are vulnerable looking for love on Internet. Both the older and younger victims let the fraudsters near and believe their lies. The scammers get their victims to act against their own best interests. Romance scams destroy many lives. They cause addiction. The recovery can take years.

Also remember that the romance scammers can lead their victims to become drug or money mules. Drug or money muling or money washing is a criminal offence. In some countries, like Singapore or Indonesia it can lead the criminal to the dead row.

New Kind of Scams, including Blackmail and Sex-Extortion:
The new blackmailing and sex-trafficking scams are often the next step from the romance scams. In them the fraudsters lead their victims to compromising actions in from of the camera. The victims let their scammers close and invitingly give them the tools to use to scam them.

Business Scams:

Scams targeting businesses use high tech spyware in order to get the target businesses to send money to wrong accounts or pay their bills several times, or lose money in some other way. It is not very surprising that the victims are found through the fraudsters personal contact networks.

Tips to prepare for online fraudsters:

If you want to know if something published on the social media is true or false, you can check it on www.snopes.com. Snopes is the oldest online site researching urban legends. The founder David Mikkelson started it in 1994. It is very popular with researchers, journalists, folklorists and those people who like to know what the truth of the matter is.

Google you own name and look for your own pictures on https://support.google.com/websearch/answer/1325808?hl=en. You get to know how your information is used there.

Always make sure that you Internet bank has a two tied security and be careful in using the public computers.

Download your files to a separate hard drive to make sure that if sometig happens to your own computer your information is protected.

When buying online, think of the following:

- Research and compare
- Check the condition of the goods and their return policy
- Keep your personal information secure
- Do not send you bank details on email
- Use a secured payment system
- Never send money to anyone you do not know personally
- If you think you have been scammed, contact your bank or the seller and report the scam

Look for information about Internet fraud and scams from reliable sources: www.RomanceScamsNow.com, https://againstromancescams.org/ (SCARS), www.thescamwatch.gov.au

If you are a victim of fraud, join a support group. Ask your police about them or join in a secure, the Society of Citizens Against Romance Scams (SCARS) approved support group online

Talk openly about fraud with your friends and family of all ages.

If you know you are being scammed, report to the police and to www.AnyScam.com

Have you asked yourself if your home insurance covers fraud as well

To prepare for the avoidance of business scams use professional help to analyse the risks of your company against fraud and fraudsters. Train your workers in recognising fraud, assess the results. Add fraud avoidance to the training list and check your insurance policies and risks.

How to be safe on social media:

1. Avoid free gifts, information and research. Scammers often offer free gift cards and sale items to get people to like certain internet or social media sites. With these scams the fraudsters want to get to the victims' social media accounts. Specifically avoid to confirm your account in order to win a price.
2. Do not accept friendship requests from people you do not know. With accepting scammers as you friends they have access to your friends as well.
3. Avoid scammers who use your friends" profiles to get to you. Always make sure by asking a friend that you already have in your list if they have started a new account.
4. Avoid scammer invented fake news and articles. They can use popular and famous company names to spread fake information for people to share.
5. Avoid scammer invented videos, movie clips and sales items. They might lead you to such internet sites that download viruses to your computer.
6. Avoid clicking on dangerous article and pictures. Often you can get viruses through clicking on the pictures of famous people.

7. Avoid oversharing. If you are in any way uncertain about the truthfulness of an article or information, do not share it.
8. Make sure the security of your social media profiles is right, so that your personal information and postings will be secure and safe.

The Five stages of the Internet Scam Victims according to The Society of Citizens against Romance Scams (SCARS):

1. Denial: 'He/she loves me, cannot be a scammer, I don't believe it, and You are a liar'
2. Anger: 'Scammers Pile of Crap, How could I be so stupid, Who does s/he think he/she is, and I demand justice'
3. Bargaining: 'Can I have my money back, someone please help me, I want to track down my scammer, and I need my money'.
4. Depression: 'I will never get my money, no one will help me, I was so dumb, and now I will give up altogether'.
5. Acceptance: 'It's sad but I have learned from it, I will never be a victim again, I will help others, support anti-scamming movement, advocate and even donate money for the course.

How to help your friends/family/acquaintance when suspecting they are being scammed:

Internet scams are potentially very traumatic experiences for the victim. The victim is often in a very deep state of denial. He/she does not believe anything you say or take in any advice from any person. Especially if it questions his or her own belief in how the romance is flowing. Friends, acquaintances and family need to be very careful and understanding, in balance with firmness, if they are really to succeed in helping the scam victim to recovery after the ordeal of being scammed. Scamming can lead to the deep trauma and shame.

The first action for those who want to help the victims of scam is to acquaintance themselves with Internet fraud, especially with romance scams openly and without prejudice. Here is some suggestions where to start:

- Do not criticize, slander or belittle you friend's scamming experience. Do not place yourself morally above him/her with statements that place yourself as immune to online fraud, in any way. Romance scam can happen to anyone. Instead become a real friend and give your support to her/him.
- Increase the level of your contacting your friend. Place yourself in her/his daily life. Call him/her every day, ask how she/he is, invite him/her to your daily hobbies or out for a coffee and visits. The victims of scams are often lonely and isolated from their own community, friends and family,
- Remember that feelings and intuition is irrational. Scam victims live filled with feelings. The scammers want them to fall in love with them as deep as possible and as quickly as possible. Give the right kind of advice:
  1. Flight tickets can be bought anywhere. It is not necessary to send money overseas for them.
  2. The Visas are not so very expensive. It all depends on the nationality. Check the right information from the immigration.
  3. Military personal in Afghanistan or anywhere in the world do not need extra money for expenses of any kind. They are free to use their own accounts any time. They do not need money for flight tickets.
  4. Sending money through Western Union or MoneyCram is risky because it very hard to be traced.
  5. Give your friend a list of red flags that are sure signs of scamming: fake ID, stolen picture, not meeting the 'lover' face-to-face, travel to Asia, especially to Dubai, sends you gifts, asks for bank details, becomes ill, a solder, an engineer, model, cannot

properly write, the weird use of gramma, widowed, has a young child, lost his wife, children or parents in an accident ect.
- Sometimes you need to place yourself between your friend and the scammer:
    1. You can go directly to your friend's bank or Western Union and explain your concern.
    2. You can contact the scammer yourself as an anonymous person by creating yourself an anonymous email address and finding out the scammers mailing address. You can send him an email because scammers get hundreds of emails. You can get answers to your letters and you can give them to your friend as proof. You do need to be careful here not to anger your friend into thinking that you are trying to take her 'lover' to yourself and away from her/him.
- Give your friend some useful links and my books to read.
    - Website: www.elinajuusola.com
    - Facebook: Author Elina Juusola
    - Twitter: @ejuusola

APPENDIX

The Journey from Pioneer to Pathfinder

Words of Wisdom from Down Under
by Gloria F Orenstein

Elina Juusola and I first met at the International Interdisciplinary Congress on Women in Haifa, Israel, in 1982. We were both scholars and feminist activists, and despite our age difference, we became fast friends and international correspondents before the era of the Internet and e-mail.

Then, in 1996, Elina and I found ourselves together again at the Fourth International Interdisciplinary Conference on Women in Adelaide, Australia. Elina had been doing research on the many forms of violence against women. She was also a feminist songwriter and would often sing from her repertoire at group meetings and evening gatherings. I learned too that she had been active in Finland, her homeland, in events for women and peace. She had written the marching song for a 10,000-person march from Helsinki to Moscow, and she sang for ten kilometres to the Helsinki Parliament House.

Although we corresponded from time to time, we lost contact with each other for a few decades. During that time, Elina had moved to Australia, where she and her family cared for her grandparents.

I had known Elina to have been a feminist entrepreneur as well as a scholar and activist. She had started a company, back in the eighties, creating Barbie and Ken dolls in antistereotypic gender roles and in innovative clothing for the next wave of feminists and pro-feminism men of the future. In 1986, she paid me a visit in Los Angeles, and among other things, we visited doll museums. I had never visited these museums, but there they were most amazing and very inspiring to Elina. She was always busy creating ways to raise the consciousness of future generations of both women and men, and she combined her activism with her scholarship and musical talent in ways that enriched all our lives. Finally, in the early nineties, Elina organized a huge exhibition where famous Finnish designers dressed the Barbie dolls. It was held at her gallery in Porvoo. Back then, she was definitely a pioneer. Surely, I believed, I would hear more about Elina in the future.

During the period of our feminist scholarship and activism, I was visited by a Sami shaman (from Samiland, Northern Norway), and I knew that Elina lived in the Finnish Lapland. Ellen Marit, my shaman, had explained to me that the northern part of the area (all of which I had thought of as Lapland) must be called Samiland because of the important Sami population found there. But more recently, Elina specified that the southern part, where she lived, must be referred to as Lapland. Elina was a Laplander. My shaman was a Sami.

One summer, when I was going to visit my shaman, Elina came to visit me in Alta, Norway. We shared many adventures in the mountains, hiking along the rim of the world with what we knew were bird spirits guiding us back to the tent so that we didn't get lost. These moments had created precious memories in our friendship. No one would ever have imagined that I, originally a New Yorker, would be trekking through the mountains near the North Pole. I had already spent five weeks in the mountains near Alta with the shaman and her father when Elina arrived. Seeing how difficult the mountain climbing and the outdoor camping were for me, Elina had a brilliant idea. "Gloria, what are you doing in these mountains anyway? Why don't you come home with me to my home in the Finnish Lapland and spend some time with my family in the city?"

She convinced me to go when she said she'd take me to a museum. She had my number, all right! Indeed, I could not resist her invitation, and I left the Norwegian Samiland a week earlier than planned that year. We also did pay a visit to the Gustaf Serlachius Museum at Mänttä in Häme. Thanks to Elina, I got introduced to a part of the Finnish

Lapland that I never would have known otherwise. I had planned to write about the Sami culture, which I had been invited to learn about with the Gaup family, but the death of two of my shaman's sons and then of Ellen Marit herself (due to a spirit war, which was the way she referred to her cancer) cut short my shamanic apprenticeship. During all my visits to Samiland, I observed the extreme difficulty of the life of a shaman. I believe that since she was the only one who was trained as a shaman by her father, with her passing, that particular lineage would not be continued. I too experienced a deep sadness and a great loss. I realized that I had been living through the darker side of Sami shamanism that summer, something they lived with constantly, for as they used to say, 'Death is always on your left shoulder.'

I did not hear from Elina for several years after these adventures, but I knew that I would find her again. Predictably, she turned up on Facebook, and we became FB friends. I learned that she had moved from Mt. Isa to Brisbane with her family and then, more recently, with her daughters to Gympie, where she now resided—from the desert to the city and back to rural lands, as she explained to me in our recent e-mail correspondence. She already had several children who were now quite grown-up, but now she also had three grandchildren. Long periods when we were out of contact with each other, punctuated by a few e-mails, continued for several more years as we each pursued our busy lives. I was a professor at USC in Los Angeles, California, and I was now retired. One day, not too long ago, I received a letter from Elina now that she had found me again via the Internet, for I, too, had lived in several different places over the intervening years.

The era of the Internet that had magically re-located and reconnected us had also caused a major crisis in Elina's life. This crisis led directly to Elina's desire to write this book, and I take great pleasure in introducing it here because it is not only a very moving story from which we learn a lot about life in the era of vast technological transformations but is also the book of a pathfinder, for Elina had to find her way out of the labyrinth of the post-traumatic stresses that the romance betrayal entailed, and as I have come to understand, she was able to emerge whole at last from the darkness of her own very real labyrinth. However, it was only recently that I was told the entire story about the problems she was having with Internet-romance scams.

I could not have imagined that Elina, the bright young scholar, creative composer, pioneer entrepreneur, and well-informed, dedicated feminist activist I had known had fallen for these scams. It seemed so unlikely that such an *awakened* mind would believe in the lies that the scammers told those they claimed to have fallen in love with. But indeed, this had happened to Elina (as it had happened to so many educated women with raised consciousnesses), and what she sought to do research on now (and to resolve both for herself and for others) was how a person as intelligent as she was could ever have fallen prey to one of these obviously too-good-to-be-true schemes played out by the scammers. How was it possible? And then, by extension, once she had fallen in love with someone who turned out to be a criminal and a liar but whose false love she had cherished, how could she heal from the terrible sadness of her betrayed and broken heart? The answers to these queries would be ones she wished to offer to the world by writing this book.

Those of you who had looked into the issue of romance scams on the Internet and who might have read personal testimonies by many of those who had suffered enormous losses of money, possessions, self-esteem, health, mental equilibrium, and love might have noticed that there weren't any books that addressed the ways women might empower themselves so that this would never happen to them again. Elina was determined to share her insights into how she ultimately transcended these traumas to other women who had also been victimized and, in addition, to create guidelines for all women to reflect upon, to practice, or to consult when they were swept off their feet by the seduction of a non-existent lover who claimed eternal and enduring devotion but just happened to be in need of a lot of money instantly in order to get out of a jam, either a medical emergency or problems crossing the border from one country to another. They would generally claim that they possessed (or else had lost) important documents, and they were on a most-urgent, secret mission and absolutely had to reach their destination. They had to pay large sums of money in order to make their way across the border given all these impediments. Usually, these scammers said were heading towards Ghana or Nigeria. They needed several thousand dollars to be sent to them—immediately—and after receiving the funds and extricating themselves from the legal and medical problems they were caught up in, they promised they were definitely going to fly to join their beloveds (read here scam victims) so that they could begin to live out their fantasy of romantic love together.

As I perused these stories and testimonies on the Internet, it seemed to me that Australia was often a centre for romance-scamming activity. Many of the testimonies came from women in Australia. But we now knew that this scam was worldwide. The criminal activity always seemed to originate from Ghana or Nigeria, where the centres of huge global scamming industries were located.

Elina's journey to the present, where I see her today as a pathfinder, in this area of research and creativity on behalf of women is innovative. Elina is committed to going through all that it takes to unravel the steps towards liberation and safety, but she always strives to take the high road in addressing the way she can heal from the hurt and yet not inflict cruelty in the form of vengeance on the perpetrator. This book is a wake-up call that requires everyone's immediate attention. Those who have been seeking a book that will enable them to find a mode of healing from such a trauma should read this book before it is too late to get free from the repercussions of an unexpected scam that they don't even suspect is already fully active in their fantasy Internet love affairs. There is a lot of information and wisdom to be gained from reading Elina's experiences, and there is much inspiration in her endeavour to write her own book that incorporates the steps she has taken in writing a short romance story or novella based on her own experience, one that she includes at the end of her book.

However, she insists that the story she will write will have a different ending. The woman she will write about will solve her crisis in such a way that her new narrative will have a happy ending. I admire the passion of her conviction that this must not end in anything but a happy ending. But how can that be achieved if she were to continually harbour vengeful feelings once the truth of the scam and all the deceit and the lies are revealed to her? It's not just the money she has paid out that upsets her so much; it's more of the pain of the lost fantasy of this incredible love that she has taken to be real that has sent her plunging into the pit of deep depression. She does not at all want to avoid the legal procedures. On the contrary, she wants to keep the relationship alive in order to give more help to the police so they can catch as many criminals as possible. But she has always been determined to create for her heroine a happy ending to the story. She wants to impart hope to her readers that this is a goal they can achieve through a number of steps that she presents in her book, which is also a manual for self-healing.

By seeking the wisdom of global cultures on alternative and non-violent modes of healing and by putting together a team of active supporters composed of family, friends, anti-fraud organizations, the police, as well as advice from the books by spiritual leaders, psychologists, and philosophers that she has used for research, she has eventually come up with an original system for rising above the darkness that has afflicted her, one that will be extremely useful to others who may fall into the same traps set by these predators.

Having understood that it was originally what she referred to as her addiction to reading romance novels that had provided the 'highs' for her when she was suffering from the deep emotional loss of her mother, which even seemed to heal the intense physical pain of fibromyalgia—at least while she was reading her romance novels—Elina realized that she had to uncover a way to reclaim her power and recognize that despite the negativity she had endured, there was enough positive remaining from the feelings of love to help her transmute the darkness into light.

The reader will also find here how her previous research has led her to recognize to what extent romance scammers have learned techniques and strategies employed in all other global industries that deal with violence against women, including rape, abduction, pornography, prostitution, and human trafficking.

What I admire so much in Elina's writing of this book, the history of her journey, is that she is fiercely committed to *not* give her own romance novella, the one that she includes at the end of this book, a negative ending. As a student not only of science and the humanities but also of spirituality and new paradigm thinking, Elina knew that she had to find a way to empower her heroine so well that the energy of her intention, expressed through writing, would catalyze a positive outcome and would resonate strongly with the reader, energizing the intelligence of resistance in future potential victims. As the new media technologies proliferate, tracking down those most vulnerable to being scammed is becoming easier for these criminals. At the same time, a new generation will be seeking love via the Internet and its many dating sites, just as Elina has. The difference now will be that this new generation will be alerted to the dangers they may fall prey to once having been awakened by the sound advice found in her book. She is convinced that her words, when infused with her powerful intent, can transform the plight of women into a completely new paradigm narrative and create a tipping point that will result in social transformation. She is truly adamant about this even though she knows intellectually that much inner work on herself has to be done in order to overcome her own heartbreak yet remain open for love again. In view of the possibility of going back online and finding other men who seem to be right for her but who may also be scammers, she has had to become a pathfinder. Her role will be to blaze that path that will open a portal to new knowledge and, thus, to an empowered, feminist, activist womanhood. The book will be the way that she can teach women to become savvy enough to refuse to comply with the demands of the scammers. She has had to write a story backed up by information from contemporary studies of the science and psychology of addiction, of the new physics, philosophy, sociology, and feminist scholarship, that will make her positive ending believable in light of all the new information and insight that has been produced since the advent of the Internet.

It takes a village, a family, a support system, a tribe, an entire community...

The impressive reliance on various community services and organizations that will work to move Elina through the phases that will lead to transformation and empowerment are not fictional but are actual communities and support groups that she has used for herself and then written about in her book. It has taken the work of the Unstoppable Women's community and the Queensland Police Fraud Recovery and Support Group to help her deal with solving the crime and apprehending the scammers as well as supporting her in another project. This other project is one of the most important discoveries on her journey, a project that has been suggested to her lovingly by one of her sons. Elina has had the wise, motherly instinct to enlist both of her sons in the identification of the scammer she has become involved with. This is intuitively what is actually recommended by writers and doctors, such as Dr. Lewis Mehl-Madrona in his book *Narrative Medicine: The Use of History and Story in the Healing Process*.[1] Dr. Mehl-Madrona, in explaining the healing methods of aboriginal peoples in various cultures, notes that their physical illnesses are often healed by storytelling within the context of a loving, supportive community. He cites cases where the ancestors and relatives are called in to join the community in the retelling of familiar folk tales relating the most fabulous, almost unbelievable triumphant endings. They may be magical fairy tales, myths, or stories spontaneously created during the gathering about how someone has healed of a fatal disease in a way that will seem impossible to believe. The figures of grandparents and relatives who are present as the story is told often add to the power of the healing that takes place. Whether real magic, a placebo effect, or the intervention of a spirit from another dimension, it doesn't matter. What is important is that these communal spiritual activities unite her supporters, and the sufficient healing energy reaches the patient in question on whom the storytelling is focused, and the healing takes place.

The surprising result is that the patient is very frequently healed, as are the heroes of the tales. Dr. Mehl-Madrona's recommendation is to utilize the storytelling powers of the entire community and, especially, the talents of the members of the family.

Elina intuitively calls upon the practical know-how of her sons, and they have actually located the false-identity scam of her Internet lover by doing research on the web. Her son Hanno has suggested a most fascinating and what I will now refer to as an alchemical formula for transforming the story she has lived through into the possibility of a new narrative, one that will heal her heartbreak and produce a positive ending.

It is this technique that I am so eager to endorse in her book because it makes use of worldwide knowledge from aboriginal peoples of a variety of cultures about how healing often takes place via storytelling in the context of a community gathering and, at times, via a ritual as well. The storytelling narrative ceremony is powerful enough to produce physical healing without resorting to the use of toxic chemicals and invasive techniques employed by mainstream Western medicine. I am also proud to endorse Elina's honesty in speaking of her son's alchemical advice on transformation because it has played such an important role in her own new story and future life. Thus, it resonates with the aboriginal wisdom that family and even members of the younger generation may, indeed, have intuitive knowledge that can assist the elders.

Indeed, in Elina's case, her son's recommendation was in complete alignment with her own intention to give the story a positive ending.

It was his wise suggestion that she should not let the negativity of the crime and the victimization she had undergone rob her of the memory of all the highs and the ecstasy that she had felt during the time when her love, blind as it was in her early innocence, was new and thrilling. It was the passion of her love for her scammer and his for her that had almost healed the pain of her fibromyalgia and given her comfort and hope to go on and live a life that she assumed would bring her enduring happiness. Her son advised her to never forget what had happened but to discard from her thoughts temporarily all that negativity, especially while doing her creative work, so that she could let the memory of the good parts of the love she had felt prevail. She should transmute those ecstatic feelings and healing energies into her writing and cling to the positive effects that they had upon her spirit, her emotions, and her health. In writing them, while separating the positive from the negative, she must not eliminate the negative completely, for one should never forget what had taken place, and criminality must absolutely be attended to by legal proceedings. Quite possibly, the fact that her son was invited to help his mother get through this crisis activated a more- intense placebo effect, stronger healing energy, and other emotional effects in Elina that actually changed both her narrative's ending and, much later, her own life story as well. Her other three children played important roles in this process as well. Her son Nillo made some impressive drawings for the book, and it is possible that they will be used in the final product. Her daughters Nelli and Henna were also involved in contributing ideas and taking part in discussions with their mother. This interaction with her close family was extremely supportive and important to the way she explored the material for the book and thought about the ending.

However, here I must add a word about happy endings. Creative writers will surely be shocked at any advice given to someone aspiring to write a novel that it is a good idea to have a happy ending in mind for the book. One is immediately concerned, especially in this case, that the author may be falling back into her addiction to romance novels, to formulaic stories and fairy-tale endings, but it is also true, in general, that this insistence on happy endings is stifling to the freedom of literary creativity. In light of the current research on crimes against women and international scams, that idea will run contrary to Elina's whole own purpose in writing the book, which is to impart an awakening of the reader to the actual statistics about the ongoing violence to women, particularly now via Internet-romance scams. One may advise Elina that the overwhelming data on crimes against women she has specialized in when she has studied pornography, rape, and violence has to be taken into account here. Can she possibly believe that given the increase in the number of these crimes, one can or, even, should write a story that will definitely have a happy ending? Naturally, Elina is aware of all this, but she remains firm in her conviction that her romance novella has to end happily. Nonetheless, it does not seem at all likely that her heroine will immediately find the answer to her romantic dreams via Internet dating sites, which have no guarantee of being safe from crime.

After her experience in writing this book, with her passion for telling her story carrying the energy of her firm intention that her story have a happy ending, I will now currently say this: we are, at present, living in a world that is undergoing a great paradigm shift, one in which a new paradigm prevails, a quantum paradigm. This is a quantum universe, where the formerly expected outcomes of encounters in the scientific world (e.g. the collision of elementary particles with one another) are no longer predictable with accuracy. We are living in a world where indeterminacy reigns, in which one particle may effect a change in another that is entangled with it and is located far across the universe. Perhaps if we take this new knowledge from science seriously and even metaphorically, the happy-ever-after ending that previously will have come under the domain of the fairy-tale ending may need to be reconsidered, for if one accepts the scientific validity of the quantum world view, one can embrace the unexpected, the unlikely, and understand that a positive outcome is quite as likely to be as valid as a negative one, even considering the current statistics on scamming (sometimes the photon is a wave and sometimes a particle). We cannot predict which with any certainty. Nothing can be predicted, but science has also shown that the presence of an observer (here I would say the intention of the writer) may have an important influence on the outcome. If our world view has gone through a cosmic shift, perhaps our recommendations for creative writers should also shift in ways that will incorporate the new paradigm outcomes as being viable, though not necessarily probable. This is one way of coming to terms with the efficacy of the system is proposed here by Elina in which she retains the integrity of her convictions throughout, insisting on using her tale-telling power to create or to manifest what seems at the very least to be highly unlikely. But science tells us that in a quantum world, this is the way reality functions down to its most fundamental physical level. There is so much more to know about quantum physics, but for the purposes of understanding Elina's desire to insist upon a happy ending, which is anathema to creative writers in general, we must also take the high road and give her credit for working her alchemy with the elements that are the most powerful to create the greatest possibility for the hoped-for outcome.

In this case, several important elements that are essential to her alchemy are also invisible but, nevertheless, real. Among the strongest invisibles are the spirits of the ancestors; the love she always feels for a man who, according to what is presented on the Internet, does not exist (because his photo is stolen from a website and his identity is not at all the one he uses); and her conviction that following her path exactly, taking guidance from the wisdom of the earth's aboriginal peoples, will induce healing, whether through actual science, magic, the intervention of healing spirits, or placebo effect. This alchemy has a millennia-long history of working, and she will tap into that power to write her book. I am happy to say that it has worked. Nevertheless, today, having read this book, we may change our position and say instead, 'If we add all the correct elements into the process described in her system, given the reality of a quantum world, where the outcome is unpredictable, it may be possible, if not likely, that with the wisdom of centuries behind the method, this may in fact bring about the desired result.'

The book goes on to develop a system for the reader to utilize in analyzing her particular narrative, its timeline, and its elements. Her feelings at different points in her story are essential to review. In addition to the system, Elina provides for us important information about the way our hormones work to induce highs and to create addiction. At different points, she has one part of her brain speak to the other. She works on herself in figuring out how it feels to be the scammer, to walk in his shoes in order to bring up some compassion for him (as if he were real, his money problems, his health issues, his legal problems. She makes the scammer into her muse. Writers have traditionally had a muse they turn to. She plays with these roles to provide a way to transform the energies of the negative into creative, healing energies. I do not want to give away anything more, to divulge the system, or to reveal her instructions on how to integrate various storylines and timelines into the new narrative. She experiments with materials drawn from her own personal experience with scamming. She writes several variants of her tale, each with different endings. But none of them are satisfactory because, as you may have begun to suspect, 'it takes two to tango.' She will have to look for a new kind of man, one who will share and support her creative life and her desire for freedom. She will be seeking a mature love based on equality and integrity. How will she go about the search while following the steps in her system?

Here is where women's studies, men's studies, gender studies, and LGBT studies come into play. In Elina's case, she is looking for a male partner, but obviously not the kind of stereotypical macho or sexist man that one may find on these websites. Who are the men she is looking for? She has begun her search by catching up on the latest writings in the new pro-feminism men's studies curricula.

Elina has also been very inspired by a book I've told her about, *Merlin Remembered*[2] by Lenny Schneir, Merlin's devoted and loving life partner. Elina has read this amazing book about how Merlin Stone, the acclaimed author of *When God Was a Woman*[3] and of many other goddess classics, has met Lenny later in life and how they have fallen in love. Lenny is a beautiful soul that has not been in touch with the feminine side of himself. He is a typical sexist male acculturated in patriarchy. Merlin is a free spirit and a pioneer in the exploration of mother goddess cultures, their history and mythology. This book is about how, through their love, Lenny has changed bit by bit. He just observes that her positions have made sense and are compassionate. He slowly becomes an ardent male feminist and a friend to goddess culture. His is one of the first dramatic examples I know of how the shift comes about in formerly sexist men. It is the shift that men have to make in order to find a new and deeper harmony in love while women follow their own path of liberation from the shackles of patriarchy. In our era pro-feminism, men have created the men's movement and have gone on to study the various diversities in male sexualities— their differences according to class, sexual and gender preference, race, ethnicity, spirituality, etc.

The magical happy ending of Elina's book is in the last version of her novella, based upon her own life. She includes it at the end of this book, a book within a book, a new narrative romance novella. Is it the result of magic, quantum reality, placebo effect, the intervention of spiritual-wisdom figures and enlightened entities, or the presence of the observer, whose energies affect the interaction of the elements to produce the unexpected. The happy ending is real in the true life of Merlin Stone and Lenny Schneir. Is it the materialization of desire? Is it *le hasard objectif* (objective or divine chance), as the surrealists have named it, or the synchronicity and alignment of two lovers creating what the surrealists have called the marvellous? For the surrealists believed that the marvellous is real! They have sought to create a surreality that will be composed of elements of the marvellous, like the fur-lined teacup (by Meret Oppenheim) or the lobster telephone (by Salvador Dalí). We can all invoke our imaginations and create a world that is surreal because, according to quantum physics, the marvellous is also real.

Ours is a world composed of the magic of the invisible intermingling with the visible, whose secret alchemical formula integrates community, storytelling, compassion, and non-violence into an alchemical medicine (in the shamanic sense of the word) whose most powerful component is another invisible but real vibration: love—love in large doses strong enough to transmute the multiple elements of the trauma into an unexpected happy ending. Elina has blazed a path through the mystery of smoke and mirrors and lifted us all out of an ongoing post-traumatic stress scenario by her utilization of ancient methods of healing. Today, new paradigm thinkers believe in the efficacy of what they have learned from the elders, their ancestors, their healers and shamans, that the vibratory resonance of words and of written stories contain healing sounds, rhythms, and storylines that echo through the ages, transmitting the vibrations necessary for the quite possible manifestation of almost unbelievable but actually true happy endings.

NOTES AND REFERENCES

Chapter 1
Introduction

1. Available through www.scamwatch.gov.au
2. Richardson, Sarah (2014). *Shocking Truth about Dating*: Guidance and advice to recognise the scam, detect the scammer and prevent becoming a victim of online fraud. The Kindle e-book edition.
3. Whitty, Monica (2012). *The Psychology of the Online Dating Romance Scam*. University of Leicester Research paper. Retrieved on 09/08/2014 from https://www2.le.ac.uk/departments/media/people/monica-whitty/Whitty_ romance_ scam_report.pdf
4. Bradley, Sabour (2014). *Heads First*. Series 1 Ep 1 Social Monster. ABC TV, Australia, rerun.
5. Bradley, Sabour (2014). *Heads First*. Series 2 ep 5 The Porn Ultimatum. ABC TV, Australia.
6. Juusola-Halonen, Elina (1985) 'Pornografia, peilikuva yhteiskuntaan [Pornography, a Mirror on Society]' *Laavunaiset 15-vuotta juhlajulkaisu*, Oulu (1986) 'Väkivallan ulottuvuudet' [The Dimensions of Violence], in *Vastarintaa*. Turku: Turun yliopiston julkaisut (Turku University prints)

Chapter 2
My Story

1. Whitty, Monica (2012) *The Psychology of the Online Dating Romance Scam*. University of Leicester Research paper. Retrieved on 09/08/2014 from https://www2.le.ac.uk/departments/media/people/monica-whitty/Whitty_ romance_ scam_report.pdf
2. It is noted here that Stephen is a fictional name I picked for the pretend character created by my scammer. The conversations are edited in order to bring the highlights as an example to the reader. I have no idea of the identity of my scammer or where he is from in real life. By googling some of the sentences, you

can find them scattered throughout the Internet. This is where the scammers source their material for the letters that work on their victims.
3. Ghana Romance Scammers community (Facebook)
4. Retrieved from http://www.male-scammers.com/the-scammers.asp?id=380 10/09/2014
5. Retrieved from http://www.male-scammers.com/the-scammers.asp?id=380 10/09/2014
6. www.police.qld.gov.au-advancefeefraud

Chapter 3
The World Through My Eyes

1. http://www.azquotes.com/quote/813502
2. Go to *Unstoppable Women Howling at the Moon* on Facebook to get more information on these monthly events in Brisbane, Australia.
3. Trenoweth, Samantha (ed) (2015) *Fury: Women Write About Sex, Power and Violence*, Melbourne: Hardie Grant Books, (Kindle edition).
4. O'Reilly, Christina (2013). *The Transformation of Love*. Self-published (currently not available).

Chapter 4
How are the Sex, Romance Book reading, and Pornography Industries Connected with the Romance Scams Industry?

1. Starhawk (1982) *Dreaming the Dark: Magic, Sex and Politics*. Boston: Beacon Press, appendix.
2. If you want to explore more on this issue, read Wolf, Naomi (2012) *Vagina: A New Biography*, London: Virago, as an introduction for female sexuality.
3. All these notes are verified true in Okun, Robe A, (ed) (2014). *Voice Male: The Untold Story of the Pro-feminist Men's Movement*. Northampton: Interlink Books, Kindle edition. Also read http://www.sydneysymposium.unsw.edu.au/2010/ chapters/DonnersteinSSSP2010.pdf
4. Heinige kommun SOU 1979:56
5. Meulenbelt, Anja (1982). *Till oss själva*. På vag till en befirad kvinnlig sexualitet. Oslo: Wahlström & Widstrand
6. Veblen, Thorstein (1899) *The Theory of the Leisure Class*. Available http://www.gutenberg.org/ebooks/833

Also (1904) *The Theory of the Business Enterprise*. Available http://www.free- ebooks.net/ebook/The-Theory-of-Business-Enterprise.

7. Lerner, Gerda (1986). *The Creation of Patriarchy*. Oxford: Oxford University Press.

[8] Just google it, but you can start from http://en.wikipedia.org/wiki/Human_Genome_Project.

Chapter 5
How to Recognise Your Belief System

[1] Jost, John T (2013). "Outgroup Favoritism and the Theory of System Justification: A Paradigm for Investigating the Effects of Socioeconomic Success on Stereotype Content" in *Cognitive Social Psychology*: The Princeton Symposium on the Legacy and Future of Social Cognition. Ed Gordon B. Moskowitz. Psychology Press.
[2] Diamond, T. G. (2009). *My Darling Davis: How Real is Your Love?* iBooks digital edition.
[3] Jost, John, (2013)
[4] Rosling, Hans and Ola (2014). "How not to be ignorant about the world." TED talk retrieved from http://www.ted.com/talks/hans_and_ola_rosling_how_not_ to_be_ignorant_about_the_world?language=en 30/09/14

Also you might want to see Steer, Andrew (2015). "How can big data help us make better decisions?" Talk at the World Economic Forum (April 10).

[5] Plato (380BC) *The Republic*. Available through Project Guttenberg on http://www.gutenberg.org/files/1497/1497-h/1497-h.htm, retrieved 30/09/2014
[6] Rousseau, Jean-Jacques (1762) *Emile or On Education*. Retrieved from http://oll. libertyfund.org/titles/2256 30/09/2014.
[7] http://en.wikipedia.org/wiki/Nikolay_Bobrikov. Retrieved 30/09/2014.
[8] http://en.wikipedia.org/wiki/Eugen_Schauman. Retrieved 30/09/2014.

Chapter 6
What to Know about the Chemistry of Love and Arousal

[1] Wolf, Naomi (2012). *Vagina: A New Biography*, London: Virago.
[2] Read for example Mel, Jonny (2013) *Dating Scam: On the Other Side*, L&L Publishing. Can be purchased as a Kindle edition.
[3] For this insight I mainly read Kessler, David D. (2010). *The End of Overeating*. London: Penguin Books (downloaded the Kindle edition)

Chapter 7
How to Use the Theory of Turning Emotion to Money and Develop a Perfect Pitch for Love for Scamming, Romance, and Pornography Industry Business

[1] Hill, Napoleon (2012). *Think and Grow Rich*. iBooks edition (original from 1937).

2. Nixon, Richard Gilly (2005) *The Lazy Man's Way to Riches, Version 3.0*. New Jersey:John Wiley & Sons, Inc.
3. Karbo, Joe (1973). *The Lazy Man's Way to Riches*. Original classic text from http:// www.what-is-coaching.com/support-files/lazymansway2riches.pdf. Retrieved 18/08/2014.
4. The original letter by Joe Karbo can be found on page 245 of Nixon's book.

Chapter 8
Why are Mature People More Vulnerable to Scamming?

1. http://faculty.georgetown.edu/tannend/sexlies.htm

Chapter 10
Thinking about Recovery through Transformative Thinking

1. Plato, *The Republic*. Jowett e-text #150 Available as a free e-book through the Guttenberg Project.
2. Mills, Joy (2000). *Entering on the Secret Way*. Wheaton: Wisdom Tradition Books.
3. Houston, Jean (2009). *A Passion for the Possible: A Guide to Realizing Your True Potential*. HarperCollins e-books.
4. www.abc.net.au/radionational/programs/latenightlive/2015-sydney-peace-prize- recepient/6388382 13/4/2015.
5. *The Telegraph*, May, 22, 2015, online edition.
6. Cole, Tillie (2014). *Raze*. Kindle eBook edition.
7. Shochet, Ian, et al (2009). *PRO, Promoting Resilient Officers*, developed by the School of Psychology and Counselling at QUT.
8. Gilbert, Elizabeth (2009). "Your elusive creative genius." TED Talk

Chapter 12
Discussion on the Possibility of Alternative Storylines through Social Change

1. Hurri, Merja ed (1986). *Naislaulukirja*. Työväen musiikki-instituutti. Helsinki: Hakapaino, Hki.
2. Lerner, Gerda: Chapter four, "The Woman Slave."
3. www.mamamia.com.au/news/boko-haram-girls -pregnant/ retrieved on 7/5/2015.
4. www.dailytelegraph.com.au/news/world/jailed-for-40-years-for-miscarrying-after-being-raped/ retrieved on 29/05/2015.
5. Okun, Rob A. (ed) (2014). *Voice Male: The Untold Story of the Pro-feminist Men's Movement*, Northampton: Interlink Books. (Kindle edition)
6. Ensler, Eve (2009). "Breaking the Secret Code of Dudes," in *Voice Male*.

⁷   Axelrod, David B; Thomas, Charol F; Schneir, Lenny (2014) *Merlin Stone Remembered: Her Life and Work*. Woodbury, Minnesota: Llewellyn Publications (Kindle edition)

Chapter 14
Concluding the Journey and Moving on with Life

¹   Van de Weyer, Robert, ed. (1998). *Rumi In a Nutshell*. London: Hodder & Stoughton.

Appendix - Words of Wisdom from Down Under by Gloria F Orenstein
The Journey from Pioneer to Pathfinder

¹   Lewis Mehl-Madrona, MD, PhD (2007) *Narrative Medicine: The Use of History and Story in the Healing Process*. Rochester: Vermont: Bear and Company
²   David B. Axelrod, Carol F. Thomas, and Lenny Schneir (2014) *Merlin Stone Remembered: Her Life and Work*. Woodbury, Minnesota: Llewellyn Publications.
³   Merlin Stone (1976) *When God Was a Woman*. New York: Houghton Mifflin Harcourt Publishing Company.